MENTAL HEALTH AMONG AFRICAN AMERICANS

Innovations in Research and Practice

Erlanger A. Turner

LEXINGTON BOOKS
Lanham • Boulder • New York • London

Published by Lexington Books
An imprint of The Rowman & Littlefield Publishing Group, Inc.
4501 Forbes Boulevard, Suite 200, Lanham, Maryland 20706
www.rowman.com

6 Tinworth Street, London SE11 5AL

British Library Cataloguing in Publication Information Available

Library of Congress Cataloging-in-Publication Data Available

ISBN 978-1-4985-6577-6 (cloth)
ISBN 978-1-4985-6578-3 (electronic)

CONTENTS

List of Figures   vii

List of Tables   ix

Acknowledgments   xi

1 Ethical Dilemmas in Psychology   1

2 Discrimination and Race-Related Stress   11

3 The Four A's of Treatment Initiation   25

4 Clinical Practice with African American Clients   39

5 African American Values   57

6 Defining the Future of Research and Clinical Practice   71

References   83

Index   93

About the Author   95

LIST OF FIGURES

Fig. 2.1   Theoretical Model of Race-Related Stress   17

Fig. 3.1   Model of Treatment Initiation for African
            Americans   27

Fig. 4.1   Layered Ecological Model of the
            Multicultural Guidelines   44

LIST OF TABLES

Table 1.1   Summary of Core Ethical Principles   9

Table 6.1   Culturally Adapted Interventions with
             African Americans   79

ACKNOWLEDGMENTS

Writing this book was a great joy and I am sure that I will forget to thank someone who has had a significant impact on my life and the completion of this book. First and foremost, I have to send a special thank you to my family for their prayers, love, and understanding. As a boy growing up in Baton Rouge, your encouragement gave me the strength and vision to reach this stage in my life and career. To my mother, Linda, your strength to push forward each day gave me the motivation I needed during hard times. There were so many days when I wanted to throw in the towel. However, when I think about you overcoming and fighting your battle with breast cancer, it gave me the extra motivation to keep pushing forward.

Second, I want to thank my cousin (Tinicia), siblings (Malanda and Darrick), and best friends (Neil, James, and Freddie) for their moral support and humor that got me through the difficult times over the last year. It meant so much to call, text, or spend time together to celebrate meeting my small writing goals along the way.

This book would not be possible without the education and training that helped to foster my growth as a professional and psychologist. I would like to thank my professors and mentors from Louisiana State University, where I earned my bachelor of science degree, and the faculty in the PhD program in clinical psychology at Texas A&M University. My skills as a mental health professional also grew tremendously while completing my postdoctoral training in clinical child psychology at the Kennedy Krieger Institute (KKI)/Johns Hopkins University

School of Medicine. Without the guidance of my clinical supervisors at KKI, I would not have been able to hone my skills working with diverse populations. I appreciate the families in inner-city Baltimore for trusting me with their well-being, sharing their lives with me, and challenging me to think more broadly about how systemic challenges negatively contribute to attending therapy. I also want to personally thank Dr. Susan Perkins-Parks, director of the KKI Behavior Management Clinic. As my first African American direct clinical supervisor, I was grateful for your mentorship, professionalism, and hospitality. It meant a lot to join your family during holidays when I could not travel to Louisiana.

Additionally, I want to thank the University of Houston-Downtown (UHD) students and my UHD colleagues for their inspiration and intellectual discussions related to diversity. Our conversations were instrumental in helping me think about how my work could be useful to reduce disparities. To my former student research assistants through my Race and Cultural Experiences (RACE) Research Lab, I am privileged to have had the opportunity to provide you with mentorship and I am indebted to you for your assistance with collecting data for my research projects and for all the hard work you did on conducting literature searches on articles for this book.

Finally, I want to thank my acquisitions editor, Kasey Beduhn, and the staff at Lexington and Rowman & Littlefield for having faith in my ability to deliver. Kasey, your kind heart and professionalism was much appreciated during my journey of writing my first book.

I

ETHICAL DILEMMAS IN PSYCHOLOGY

Psychology as a science has been pivotal in understanding human behavior, shaping public policy, and improving the lives of society. However, the field of psychology has not always been on the positive side of change. Early work by psychologists and scientists was published with the intent to advance knowledge but often resulted in negative effects on African Americans and marginalized groups as a result of unethical behavior (Grier & Cobbs, 1968; Sinclair, 2017; Turner, Malone, & Douglas, 2019). Before the unethical behavior associated with the well-known Tuskegee syphilis study, science was also used to attribute low intellectual functioning to race, to support efforts to sterilize groups of people through the use of eugenics, and to support slavery (Guthrie, 1976; Sinclair, 2017). According to Sinclair (2017), early research that was published reflected "what we would now see as a misuse of science and had little awareness of the harm that could be done by prejudicial beliefs and a lack of acknowledgment of social justice issues." However, Guthrie (1976) states that pseudoscience in the field of psychology and anthropology heavily contributed to notions that one race was "inherently superior to another." The majority of research during the nineteenth century did not address the need for ethical responsibility nor was consideration given to the need for ethical guidelines.

This chapter focuses on understanding the importance of ethical responsibility, reviews historical perspectives on unethical behavior, and provides an overview of best practices for engaging in ethical behavior when working with individuals from diverse groups. It also provides some specific considerations for working with African Americans. Throughout this chapter and the book, it is important to recognize within-group differences, with respect to African Americans. In future chapters, more discussion is provided on cultural competence and an Afrocentric perspective.

HISTORICAL PERSPECTIVE AND ETHICAL ISSUES

Ethical responsibility is important for the advancement of science, for the protection of human rights, and to increase participation in research. If history has taught us anything, we know that science has a strong impact on our society. One of the most important reasons for ethical codes and guidelines is for the protection of the public and research participants. Ethical responsibility is necessary to advance science and to ensure that participants can adequately make an informed decision about engaging in research or seeking psychological treatment. To advance the field and prevent future unethical behavior, it is necessary that we have a clear understanding of past unethical behavior and harm that has been caused by the health profession. Understanding the role of science in historical mistreatment of society (e.g., genocide, slavery, and colonization) is valuable and should be central to the engagement of our work with individuals from racial and ethnic groups (Bernal & Adames, 2017).

According to Koocher and Keith-Spiegel (2008), ethical violations typically represent three broad categories: (a) competence issues, (b) lack of or lapses in maintaining self-awareness, and (c) insensitivity. As detailed in numerous past unethical situations, individuals working in the fields of psychology and medicine often misrepresented their professional responsibility at the disadvantage of African Americans or other marginalized groups. Whether in research studies or clinical settings, ethical misbehavior can have short- or long-term effects on both the profession and the communities that they serve. Incompetence by professionals may include issues such as lacking sufficient knowledge about ethical guidelines and standards or lacking an adequate skill set for working with a particular group of people (e.g., African American clients). Errors in self-awareness are known to result in rationalizing decisions and behaviors based on one's own biases

(Koocher & Keith-Spiegel, 2008; Pope & Vasquez, 2016). Finally, insensitivity patterns may lead professionals to have tunnel vision and solely focus on identifying patterns that support their own biases. Koocher and Keith-Spiegel (2008) note that insensitivity could include lack of empathy, self-absorption, and prejudicial attitudes toward certain people. In hindsight, it is easy to identify clear examples of ethical violations based on these categories of unethical behavior.

Numerous scholars from professions such as psychology, social work, anthropology, and medicine have discussed the historical mishaps within their content area. Trimble, Scharrón-del Río, and Casillas (2014) note that for many people, the term "research" has a negative connotation and is linked to European imperialism and colonialism. This has often resulted in many ethnic and racial communities being suspicious of researchers. Individuals from ethnocultural communities (e.g., Native American and African American) are "often unforgiving of past research efforts that left them feeling harmed or exploited" (Trimble, Scharrón-del Río, & Casillas, 2014). For example, it has been recognized that many African Americans in the United States have worked to overcome their history of oppression as a result of centuries of slavery, decades of Jim Crow laws, human experimentation, and devaluing of Black life (Turner, Malone, & Douglas, 2019).

Although not the first misuse of science with African Americans, the Tuskegee syphilis study is one of the most well-known experiences to highlight the need for ethical responsibility. In the syphilis study, African American men living in Alabama were recruited to participate in a study to examine "bad blood" and were coerced into continued participation in the study without proper informed consent or the option to discontinue participation (Guthrie, 1976; Suite et al., 2007; Trimble, Scharrón-del Río, & Casillas, 2014). This study highlights the absence of ethical practice that guides research investigations today (Trimble, Scharrón-del Río, & Casillas, 2014). Trimble and colleagues (2014) hypothesize that one of the reasons for unethical behavior in conducting research is due to assumptions about power and science that are shaped by inequality; to change this perspective and prevent future errors researchers must move away from this thinking especially when doing research with ethnocultural communities. The syphilis experiment has left a lasting impact on many African Americans openness to engage in research and seek mental health treatment.

Outside of the United States, ethical conduct by scientists and researchers has also been called into question due to enabling oppression and mistreatment of society. Vasquez (2012) describes how psychological science was used in South Africa to help structure and maintain apartheid. Another example of unethical behavior at the cost of advancing science occurred in Guatemala. The study's primary investigator, John Cutler, intentionally infected Guatemalan people (prisoners, soldiers, and mental health patients) with syphilis, gonorrhea, and chancroid (Reverby, 2012; Trimble, Scharrón-del Río, & Casillas, 2014). Ironically, Cutler was also one of the researchers involved in the Tuskegee syphilis study. To move forward as a profession, scholars stress the significance of how we apply psychological knowledge on the communities that we serve and/or use as research participants (Bernal & Adames, 2017; Pope & Vasquez, 2016; Trimble, Scharrón-del Río, & Casillas, 2014; Vasquez, 2012).

THE IMPORTANCE OF ETHICS IN RESEARCH AND PRACTICE

Ethical codes and guidelines are generally intended to provide guidance to a profession on how individuals should conduct themselves. We assign judgments to behavior as "right" or "wrong" and "good" or "bad" according to some socially accepted guideline (Koocher & Keith-Spiegel, 2008). One of the earliest codes or guidelines to address ethical concerns was the Nuremberg Code. The *Nuremberg Code of Ethics in Medical Research* was created in 1947 to provide ethical guidelines for research in response to harm that resulted from experiments conducted by physicians in concentrations camps (Sinclair, 2017). Subsequently, the American Psychological Association (APA) formed a committee to address ethical behavior of psychologists. In 1959, the APA Council of Representatives adopted as APA policy a set of ethical standards for psychology that spearheaded other organizations in developing their own code of ethics (as cited in Sinclair, 2017).

To date, several professional organizations have codes of ethical conduct to help guide professional activities. You should refer to your respective professional organization to become aware of its ethics code for guidance (e.g., National Association for Social Workers, American

Counseling Association [ACA]; and American Association for Marriage and Family Therapy [AAMFT]). Specific to the field of psychology, the APA has published the *Ethical Principles of Psychologists and Code of Conduct* (APA, 2017a), *Guidelines for Providers of Psychological Services to Ethnic, Linguistic, and Culturally Diverse Populations* (APA, 1990), and *Multicultural Guidelines: An Ecological Approach to Context, Identity, and Intersectionality* (APA, 2017c) to assist researchers, educators, and practitioners with engaging in ethical responsibility. Although not required for use by professionals outside of psychology, the basic principles that are discussed may be applicable to working with diverse groups including African Americans. In 2015, the APA established a task force to create an additional set of guidelines for working with ethnic and racial groups. These competency guidelines are particularly useful for expanding working with African Americans.

Whereas the guidelines published by professional organizations are helpful to provide general rules of conduct, some speculate that current ethics codes are too simplified. According to Koocher and Keith-Spiegel (2008), the existing ethical regulations are not set up to handle the complexities of conducting research with diverse ethnic populations and these guidelines are insufficient for navigating research with youth from racial and ethnic backgrounds. Others posit that unethical conduct continues among researchers due to the process of "othering," which places knowledge, power, and expertise on the researcher, therefore the researcher decides what to study and how the study should be conducted (Trimble, Scharrón-del Río, & Casillas, 2014). Koocher and Keith-Spiegel (2008) provide a detailed list of examples of unethical behaviors when conducting research such as falsification of data, not supervising research assistants, and failure to follow scientific regulations. As previously noted, several professional organizations (e.g., APA, AAMFT, and ACA) also provide ethical guidelines for clinical practice.

One of the earliest studies to document ethical dilemmas among psychologists was conducted by Haas, Malouf, and Mayerson (1986). The authors examined practitioners' perceptions of ethical dilemmas by using a series of 10 ethical vignettes that represented general categories of professional issues including confidentiality, informed consent, loyalty conflicts, exploitation, and whistleblowing (i.e., reporting unethical behavior of a colleague). Using a sample of 294 psychologists (91% PhD or PsyD; 70% male), results indicated that the highest consensus (at least 75% agreement) regarding the appropriate ethical decisions were obtained on issues involving conflicts of interest, mandatory reporting of threatened violence, referring a client to someone who is considered incompetent, and confidentiality. Furthermore, less agreement was found for dilemmas involving the use of professional credentials in advertising for local businesses, providing treatment for problems beyond one's expertise, and reporting potential clients' therapeutic diagnoses to insurance companies. Interestingly, the study also found that a majority of respondents would not report allegations of sexual abuse but instead would try to encourage the client or a family member of the client to make that report. According to the authors (Haas, Malouf, & Mayerson, 1986), despite the increasing prevalence of mandatory reporting laws, the results show that uncertainty about this complex ethical issue is widespread. Although this work sheds some light into professional dilemmas faced by mental health professionals, one of the limitations of this study was that the authors "forced" respondents to answer in a particular way given the use of closed-ended questions.

In general, members of professional organizations (e.g., APA, ACA, etc.) see a huge benefit in how ethical guidelines help them to navigate their work (Pope, Tabachnick, & Keith-Spiegel, 1987; Pope & Vetter, 1992). For example, one study (Pope, Tabachnick, & Keith-Spiegel, 1987) conducted to understand ethical practices and knowledge among psychologists found that members oftentimes report that the following sources were rated as "good" or "excellent" sources of information on ethical responsibility: internships and graduate programs, APA ethical principles, APA Ethics Committee, continuing education programs, and informal networks and colleagues. Based on this data, it is not surprising that the APA code of ethics is considered to be an important resource for mental health professionals and psychologists. The study also indicated that psychologists rated the following as adequate sources of information: agencies where they worked, state and federal laws, state licensing boards, local and state ethics committees, and published research on theoretical and clinical practice (Pope, Tabachnick, & Keith-Spiegel, 1987). Although this work provides some insight into psychologists' experience, one limitation of this study (Pope, Tabachnick, & Keith-Spiegel, 1987) is that it only gathered information from one segment of psychology professionals.

More recently, Pope and Vetter (1992) conducted a study to gather data from a representative sample (n = 679) of mental health professionals (i.e., psychologists) to understand the types of ethical issues faced in their clinical work. The results indicated that participants endorsed a total of 703 ethical incidents that were divided into 23 general categories with the most common troubling incidents including confidentiality (n = 128; 18%), dual relationship (n = 116; 17%), and payment/fee issues (n = 97; 14%). Additionally, the authors reported that the most troubling or challenging incidents related to confidentiality involved 38 instances of disclosing information to third parties, 23 involving child abuse reporting, and 6 involving patients who threatened or had committed violence. In terms of issues around boundaries in multiple relationships, participants in the study reported that in some situations it is challenging to identify what is and what is not considered a dual relationship. The authors (Pope & Vetter, 1992) concluded that the data suggests that the ethical principles need to define dual relationships more carefully and to provide clarity on if and when a dual relationship is therapeutically indicated or acceptable. This may be particularly important for mental health providers that provide services to African Americans due to either working in a small community or living in a neighborhood where there is high probability of a dual relationship. For example, given some African Americans' preferences for a provider of the same race, they may have previous knowledge of that provider either through their church community or a social organization.

Furthermore, it is important to recognize the role that race and ethnicity continue to play in society and how ethical practice may be influenced by mental health professionals' biased assumptions and perceptions (Arredondo & Toporek, 2004). Bernal and Adames (2017) note that it is important for mental health professionals to have an understanding of legacies of oppression and their impact on treatment. As discussed later in the text, when working with racially and ethnically diverse clients, we must be cognizant of how our biases and Western assumptions may lead to additional ethical dilemmas. Therefore, cultural competence is necessary to reduce potential liability and harm to clients. Bernal and Adames (2017) describe three ethical considerations that should be addressed when working with individuals from ethnic and racial groups: (a) apply a cultural view or perspective to evaluating the risk and benefits of an intervention, (b) apply respectful and culturally informed consent procedures with respect to confidentiality, and (c) engage in "principled cultural sensitivity"—approaches to research and intervention should not intrude or disrupt cultural values and norms. These ethical dimensions of multicultural sensitivity have been identified to help researchers improve their work with developing treatment interventions. According to Bernal and Adames (2017), by applying these dimensions in our work, it allows for using an ecological systems approach that values the client's history, culture, and environmental context. Not only does it help to reduce ethical issues in research and practice, these steps are helpful with improving cultural competence or sensitivity.

KEY ETHICAL CONSIDERATIONS

Gilligan (1982) stresses the importance of establishing and valuing relationships as the core of research, and one should be concerned about the welfare and dignity of others (as cited Trimble, Scharrón-del Río, & Casillas, 2014). I would agree with this philosophy and also emphasize how those concepts are important to consider when doing clinical work. As noted above, one should actively seek to stay aware of ethical principles when engaging in their professional roles. Table 1.1 provides a summary of core ethical principles to guide your work in clinical and research settings. To improve cultural sensitivity and ethical responsibility when working with African Americans, providers should not only abide by existing ethical guidelines but they need to consider integrating components of African American cultural values (as discussed later in the text). For example, to enhance our ability to work with African Americans, we need to be more collaborative. This is consistent with African Americans' cultural values, which focus on communalism or connectedness. Communalism has been defined as the interdependence of people and placing a value on interpersonal relationships (Boykins, Jagers, Ellison, & Albury, 1997). Gooden and McMahon (2016) note that communalism may help to promote positive outcomes such as moral reasoning. By integrating communalism in your practice, it can help to enhance rapport and demonstrate that you are concerned about the well-being of African American clients. This might also reduce the risk of unethical behavior.

One important ethical consideration is being aware of potential risks and balancing decisions around clinical work based on your own level of education, training, and experience with specific populations. Avoiding potential risk does not equal ethical practice (Koocher & Keith-Spiegel, 2008). When engaging in clinical work or conducting research, you should be concerned about how unethical behavior or harm could result when researchers or mental health professionals misinterpret, pathologize, or misidentify thoughts, emotions, and behaviors of participants or clients (Pope & Vasquez, 2016; Trimble, Scharrón-del Río, & Casillas, 2014). One method to reduce risk and ethical dilemmas is by forming partnerships with community members who could then assist with your understanding of privacy, resistance to being included in

Table 1.1. Summary of Core Ethical Principles

Do no harm	The APA code of ethics states that professionals strive to benefit the people they serve and minimize potential to inflict harm. Furthermore, professionals should be aware of their own physical and mental health and ensure that their ability to help others is not impaired.
Respect autonomy	Professionals should respect how people decide to live and respect cultural, individual, and role differences of the people they work with.
Act justly	The APA code of ethics states that professionals recognize that fairness and justice are entitled to everyone; professionals should take reasonable actions to ensure fair and equitable treatment of individuals.
Exhibit integrity	Professionals should act with fidelity, loyalty, and truthfulness in their roles as scientists, educators, and practitioners.
Act benevolently	The APA code of ethics states that professionals should be aware of how their judgments and behaviors affect the lives of others; professionals should strive to maintain appropriate boundaries and treat clients with compassion.
Exhibit accountability	Professionals should be aware of how their behaviors affect others and should take responsibility to correct any unethical actions or mistrust that results from their action or inaction.
Be courageous	Professionals should take actions to maintain trust and abide by ethical principles including reporting unethical behavior of colleagues.
Pursue excellence	Professionals should seek to maintain competence in conducting research, teaching, and doing clinical work.

Sources: APA (2017a) and Koocher & Keith-Spiegel (2008).

research, and understanding cultural meanings of the variables that we study (Koocher & Keith-Spiegel, 2008). In addition to guidelines from professional organizations, U.S. federal regulations also specify rules for conducting research with specific populations including children, those incarcerated, pregnant women, and vulnerable groups (e.g., those with a mental disability). According to Koocher and Keith-Spiegel (2008), prejudices, overriding personal needs, rationalizations, and insufficient training and experience are common culprits responsible for biased conclusions, bad decisions, and unethical behavior.

CONCLUSION

The field of psychological science and mental health has progressed substantially since its inception. Over approximately 50 years, we have a better understanding of ethical mistakes and more knowledge regarding standards of ethical behavior for both research scientists and practitioners. These advances have helped to limit the possibility that researchers and health professionals harm members of the public. However, because we as humans are infallible, it is important for us to stay vigilant in our efforts to prevent unethical behavior. Scholars also continue to stress the importance of considering how our work as scientists and clinicians must take into consideration the ethnic and cultural background of the people that we interact with to ensure the best interest of those groups and to be mindful of the influence of our research on society.

2

DISCRIMINATION AND RACE-RELATED STRESS

For many African Americans, living in the United States under racial tension can lead to mental health challenges and stress. In a report published by the American Psychological Association (APA, 2017b), the authors noted that stress is often higher in individuals from ethnic and racial groups and those from lower socioeconomic status backgrounds. Stress is more likely to result when an individual experiences high-intensity demands that are unpredictable, uncontrollable, or dangerous (APA, 2017b). Given the history of marginalization and negative life events experienced by African Americans such as exposure to discrimination, many are at higher risk of developing a mental health disorder. This is particularly concerning because research indicates that African Americans are often reluctant to seek mental health treatment (Turner et al., 2019; Williams et al., 2014). According to Belgrave and Allison (2014), racism and race relations not only influence African Americans but also affect other groups, including Whites. This chapter discusses the impact of discrimination and racism on the mental health of African Americans. Specifically, the chapter describes how experiences of racism in society can lead to poor mental health outcomes. Racism and discrimination not only increases risk of psychological difficulties, but there is also potential for higher chronic health conditions such as cardiovascular disease as a result of experiencing or perceiving racism (Belgrave & Allison, 2014).

PERCEPTIONS OF RACISM

Several authors have articulated the various types of racism that can contribute to negative outcomes for African Americans (e.g., Belgrave & Allison, 2014; Bryant-Davis et al., 2017; Bryant-Davis & Ocampo, 2005). Belgrave and Allison (2014) define racism as "attitudes, institutional arrangements, and acts that tend to denigrate individuals or groups because of phenotypic characteristics or ethnic group affiliation." Furthermore, subtypes of racism may include individual level racism, which is synonymous with racial prejudice (assuming that one's self is superior to other races); institutional racism, which is revealed in and practiced within organizations and institutions leading to discrimination of groups of people; and cultural racism, which is seen in the assumed superiority of a language or dialect, values, beliefs, worldviews, and cultural artifacts that dominate in a society (Belgrave & Allison, 2014; Carter, 2007). Racism can be traumatic and can occur after experiences such as verbal name-calling or insults, mistreatment (microaggressions), hate crimes, or physical violence (Williams et al., 2014). Given the potential for African Americans to experience racism and discrimination, it is important for mental health providers to validate these concerns and offer interventions to reduce the burden that may result from experiencing racism.

Mental health professionals may not be aware of the effects of racism on psychopathology because of a societal tendency to deny the presences of racism (Williams et al., 2014). However, there is a substantial amount of literature documenting the correlations between racism and poor mental health. Williams and colleagues (2014) state that studies have linked racism to mental health issues such as depression, substance use, and general distress. Others identify consequences such as African Americans being disproportionately represented in the justice system, being more frequently stopped by police, and poor health outcomes such as shorter life expectancies, higher rates of heart disease, and less access to mental health and healthcare services (APA, 2017b; Belgrave & Allison, 2014; Klonoff, Landrine, & Ullman, 1996). Research has also reported that people interpret or perceive racism and discrimination differently. As a result of individual differences in the perceptions of racism, it is difficult to assess consistent negative outcomes. As noted below, despite how people perceive racism, it continues to impact their mental health or physiological symptoms.

Regardless of where we live or the decade they we were born, most of us are aware of the historical nature of racism in America. Racism has historically had negative consequences for African Americans. Despite the progress that we have made as a society there remains discrimination and racism in many communities. Research has demonstrated that African Americans continue to experience discrimination whether through direct interactions or through institutions such as schools or health-care settings (Klonoff, Landrine, & Ullman, 1996). In the last 10 years, there has also been an increase in victimization and violence against African Americans by law enforcement (Bor et al., 2018; Hurst et al., 2017). This dehumanization can also result in poor mental health. For example, Bryant-Davis and colleagues (2017) noted that racial and ethnic minorities who observe or experience police brutality often experience flashbacks, nightmares, or hypervigilance. Due to the frequency of indirectly or directly experiencing racism, many African Americans may report depression, anxiety, or anger about racism, which are some of the most common problems presented by African Americans when they are seeking mental health treatment (Klonoff, Landrine, & Ullman, 1996). Counselors and mental health professionals must recognize the psychological impact of racism and perceived discrimination on African Americans (Thompson, 1996). As noted later in this book, to engage in culturally sensitive treatment, professionals must not avoid conversations around racial issues. Otherwise, it could rupture the therapeutic alliance and lead to treatment dropout.

Racism and discrimination impacts the functioning of African Americans across the developmental life span. A significant amount of literature discusses the negative influence of racism on outcomes for children and adolescents as well as young adults. Studies have found that African American youth who encounter discrimination and racism experience poor psychosocial outcomes such as low self-esteem and symptoms of depression (Harris-Britt et al., 2007). Using data from the National Survey of American Life (NSAL), Seaton, Caldwell, Sellers, and Jackson (2008) examined discrimination among African American and Caribbean Black youth to understand the consequences of discrimination on their psychological well-being. The study found that 87 percent of African American youth and 90 percent of Caribbean Black youth indicated that they had experienced at least one discriminatory incident in the past year. The authors also reported that perceived discrimination was associated with increased depressive symptoms, decreased self-esteem, and decreased life satisfaction for both groups. This work emphasizes that regardless of your ethnic identification (e.g., African American or Caribbean), being Black in America leads to increased risk for negative psychological outcomes. Furthermore, some research indicates that when parents discuss potential discrimination and prepare their children regarding society's negative bias toward African Americans, those youth are more likely to have higher academic functioning, stronger self-efficacy, and fewer depressive symptoms (Harris-Britt et al., 2007). However, the findings are mixed regarding how racial socialization may serve as a protective factor against the negative influences of racism.

Among young adults and college students, research also describes the impact of racism and discrimination on psychological outcomes. For example, many African Americans may report difficulties related to imposter syndrome. Numerous scholars identify imposter phenomenon (IP) as the feelings of intellectual incompetence experienced by some high achieving individuals (Bernard et al., 2017; Cokley et al., 2013). According to Bernard and his colleagues (2017), IP has been linked to a host of negative psychological outcomes among African American college students. Recurrent experiences of racial discrimination may also increase vulnerabilities for feelings of IP by decreasing self-esteem and self-efficacy (Bernard et al., 2017). Using a sample of college students (ages 18–21), a recent study found that racial identity and gender influenced the negative effects of IP and discrimination (Bernard et al., 2017). Specifically, the authors reported that among African American females (but not males), discrimination and IP were associated with increased depressive symptoms. Based on the cumulative evidence, it is clear that discrimination is associated with multiple negative psychological outcomes.

RACE-RELATED STRESS

Research over the last decade has discussed how race-related stress or race-based traumatic stress impacts African Americans (e.g., Bryant-

Davis & Ocampo, 2005; Williams et al., 2018). As early as the late 1960s, scholars have discussed how exposure to racism in society leads to suspiciousness, distress, and anger among African Americans (Grier & Cobbs, 1968). These experiences have been referred to by several terms including race-related stress, racial trauma, racism-related traumatic experiences, and race-based traumatic stress injury (e.g., Bryant-Davis & Ocampo, 2005; Carter, 2007; Williams et al., 2014). For the purpose of this book, the terms race-related stress, racial trauma, and race-based traumatic stress are used interchangeably. In terms of the DSM, no current psychological disorder is included that represents race-based traumatic stress. Carter (2007) and Williams and colleagues (2018) also noted that the current version of the DSM does not appropriately provide information to assess or identify race-related stress within the scope of the post-traumatic stress disorder (PTSD) symptomatology. As discussed later, several scholars have proposed methodology for assessment and identification of race-based traumatic stress (see Carter, 2007; and Williams et al., 2018 for a complete description).

Although there is no current diagnostic system recognizing a non-pathological reaction or psychiatric disorder based on experiencing racist events, that should not invalidate individuals' emotional reactions that they experience subsequent to having a racist encounter. Many scholars have discussed how discrimination and racism may lead to emotional difficulties and increased rates of PTSD among African Americans (e.g., Helms, Nicolas, & Green, 2010; Williams et al., 2014). Our current understanding of PTSD criteria is that it must result from a physical or life-threatening situation. This does not capture emotional reactions that may result from racism or discrimination. In 2018, the American Psychological Association produced a video on racism in America that highlights the psychological impact of race-related stress on African Americans (APA, 2018). In general, scholars define race-related stress or race-based traumatic stress as a psychological or emotional response following acute or chronic exposure to racism or discrimination (e.g., Carter, 2007; Helms, Nicolas, & Green, 2010; Williams et al., 2018). The following section will highlights some of the current knowledge in this area.

To understand the significance of how racism and discrimination lead to psychological difficulties, we must consider the decades of research that articulate the depth of the difficulties that are experienced by African Americans. Carter (2007) suggests that we need to consider racism as a form of psychological injury. To advance our understanding of this phenomenon, we need to improve our understanding of how race-based encounters and experiences produce psychological injury (Carter, 2007). Although research has provided evidence that exposure to discrimination and racist events lead to symptoms of race-based traumatic stress (e.g., anxiety or increased blood pressure), little is known about what aspects of racism may produce trauma (Carter, 2007). Bryant-Davis and Ocampo (2005) emphasize that experiences of racism or racist encounters are similar to traumatic experiences such as rape or domestic violence. These racist encounters may be verbal attacks, physical attacks, or threats, but because they are racially motivated, they have the potential to result in psychological distress (Bryant-Davis & Ocampo, 2005). Others note that race-based traumatic experiences can range from frequent microaggressions to blatant hate crimes and physical assault (Williams et al., 2014).

According to Scurfield and Mackey (2001), the onset of exposure to psychological injury may take three forms including discrete single incidents or repeated experiences, subtle and covert racism, and insidious exposure that involves chronic and pervasive exposure to racism. Carter (2007) states that nonpathological race-based traumatic stress injury involves emotional or physical pain or threat of physical and emotional pain that results from racism, which may be in the form of racial harassment, racial discrimination, or discriminatory harassment. Furthermore, before racism can lead to race-based traumatic stress, the individual must experience psychological stress or assault that results from one powerful racist incident that triggers the racial trauma or more subtle and prolonged trauma with a "last-straw experience" that increases the level of stress to the threshold of trauma (Carter, 2007). Individuals may experience a variety of symptoms following racist encounters. The literature indicates that race-based traumatic stress may include having reactions of intrusion, avoidance of stimuli associated with the trauma, and increased arousal or hypervigilance (e.g., Carter, 2007; Bryant-Davis & Ocampo, 2005; Williams et al., 2018). Figure 2.1 describes a theoretical model of race-related stressed based on the accumulation of research. It is important to recognize that not every African American who experiences a racist encounter will develop race-related stress or race-based traumatic stress (Bryant-Davis & Ocampo,

2005; Carter, 2007). As depicted in figure 2.1, once an individual experiences a racist encounter (e.g., being pulled over by the police), the individual must then interpret the situation negatively and have some processing of the incident over an extended period of time. After experiencing memories of the encounter and negative experience, it can then lead to possible symptoms of race-related stress.

Studies show that the nature of racism in America has many negative outcomes for African Americans regardless of the type of racism they experience. As noted earlier, racism may be experienced individually or within institutions and systems. Franklin-Jackson and Carter (2007) report that encounters of racism lead to a variety of psychological concerns including cultural mistrust, anxiety, trauma, depression, and decreased life satisfaction. Furthermore, ethnic identity or how a Black person identifies with his or her ethnic group may shape their perceptions of individual, institutional, or cultural race-related events (Franklin-Jackson & Carter, 2007; Helms, Nicolas, & Green, 2010). Using a sample of 255 African Americans, Franklin-Jackson and Carter (2007) found that race-related stress and socioeconomic status accounted for 9 percent of the variance in psychological distress. More specifically, the authors noted that individuals' race-related stress was positively related

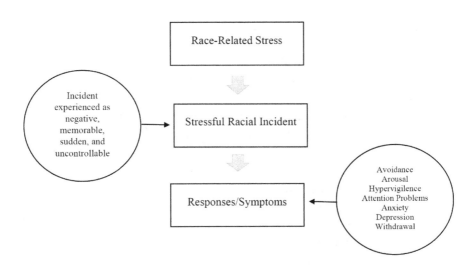

Figure 2.1.   Theoretical Model of Race-Related Stress

Source: **Author generated from Carter (2007) and Williams et al. (2018).**

to psychological distress, and socioeconomic status was significantly negatively related to psychological distress. In terms of the influence of ethnic identification, the study reported that those who identified higher levels of pre-encounter status (i.e., more acculturated to American/White values) reported more psychological distress compared to those who identified higher internalization status (i.e., secure African American identity).

Similar findings have been found among African American youth and young adults. In a study conducted by Sellers and Shelton (2003), the authors found that 38 percent of college students reported experiencing at least one encounter of racial discrimination in the past year. The authors also reported that there was a direct link between racial discrimination and poor mental health. Specifically, the study reported that experiencing racial discrimination was associated with more stress and increased risk for anxiety and depression. Sellers and Shelton (2003) also noted that the more an individual identified race as being central to the identity, less likely they were to endorse psychological distress after he or she experienced discrimination. Given these findings, it is clear that race-based traumatic stress needs to be further explored in clinical settings.

POLICE BRUTALITY AND MENTAL HEALTH

Police brutality and the murder of African Americans is not a recent phenomenon (Bryant-Davis et al., 2017; Hurst et al., 2017). Holmes (2000) broadly defines police brutality as abusive police practices that may involve abusive language, racial slurs, unnecessary searches, or physical violence that is justified to accomplish a police duty. One of the earliest and the most memorable cases of police brutality was the beating of Rodney King in Los Angeles in the 1990s. The video of the four policemen beating King was publicized by the media and confirmed what many in the African American community had previously known regarding the mistreatment of community members by law enforcement. Hurst and colleagues (2017) note that state-sanctioned police violence against African Americans represents manifestations of institutional racism, wherein policies and practices often have negative impacts on the community. This remains the case with the more recent shootings of Black males such as Tamir Rice, Alton Sterling, and Philando Castille. As one might expect, police brutality and the killing of African American males does not impact only the families of those individuals. Many African Americans have experienced negative psychological outcomes as a result of indirectly witnessing these incidents in their community and nationally on the television or through social media (May & Wisco, 2015).

Some scholars noted that race-related microaggressions have a cumulative psychological impact on African Americans across the developmental life span (Helms, Nicolas, & Green, 2010; Utsey & Payne, 2000). Studies show that racism and discrimination are associated with significant negative outcomes including hypertension, coronary heart disease, cancer, lung ailments, and cirrhosis of the liver (e.g., APA, 2017b; Utsey & Payne, 2000). Furthermore, coping with racism requires a significant amount of energy. Building on this theoretical framework of a race-related stress model by Outlaw (1993), racism is a chronic source of stress that permeates many aspects of life for African Americans and results in psychological stress responses including depression, anxiety, anger, and intense feelings of distress (as cited by Utsey & Payne, 2000). According to Utsey and Payne (2000), the cognitive energy associated with negotiating the complexities of racism in everyday life is particularly detrimental to the psychological health of African American males.

Using a sample of 126 African American men, Utsey and Payne (2000) examined the differential impact of racism on their psychological well-being. The study found that African American men had similar experiences with everyday racism and similar levels of race-related stress. However, there were differences in the psychological and emotional reactions to the chronic stress associated with everyday racism. Specifically, the authors reported that in the clinical subsample of African American men, race-related stress accounted for 16 percent of the total variance in anxiety symptoms. The authors suggested that there are some factors such as social support or internal factors (e.g., coping styles) that reduce the risk of negative outcomes for some individuals who experience racism. As previously discussed, it is possible that ethnic identity and racial socialization may influence how individuals interpret racial encounters.

Given the current knowledge of the field, the cumulative effects of experiencing a racial encounter may lead some to develop more chronic trauma or race-related stress. Continuous exposure to images of black and brown bodies lying in the street can have dramatic effects on the mental health of African Americans—especially those who have not experienced the violence directly (Hurst et al., 2017). Police shootings of African American males could be considered community violence or a shared trauma. Community violence has been defined by some as the intentional, malevolent environments that occurs outside the home, within a defined community, and perpetrated by someone other than a loved one (Galovski et al., 2016). Numerous studies examining reactions to community violence show clear relationships between exposure to community violence and psychological distress such as posttraumatic distress disorder and depressive symptoms (Bryant-Davis et al., 2017; Galovski et al., 2016).

Police brutality occurs within the context of police officers possessing privilege and often assumed justification for their actions as they have sworn to protect and serve the community (Bryant-Davi et al., 2017). Recent studies on community violence and witnessing police shootings have demonstrated the negative effects on African Americans. One study (Galovski et al., 2016) examined mental health reactions following the Ferguson shooting among members of law enforcement and community members. Results indicated that community members reported significantly higher levels of PTSD symptoms and depression compared to law enforcement. More importantly, the study found that African American community members reported significantly higher scores than White community members (with scores elevated above clinical cutoffs).

Using a large population-based sample, Bor et al (2018) examined the effects of police shootings on the mental health functioning of Americans (both White and Black). The study found that exposure to one or more police killing of unarmed Black men was associated with an increase in poor mental health days. Not surprisingly, the study reported that exposure to police killings of unarmed Black Americans was not associated with changes in mental health among White Americans. The authors concluded that the data suggested that police killings of unarmed Black Americans have a meaningful population-level impact on the mental health of Black Americans. The results of the study also support the idea of shared trauma following police shootings for African Americans. According to Bor and collegues (2018), because many of the police shootings received nationwide media coverage (or went viral on social media), there might have been spillover effects of police killings on the mental health among Black Americans living in other states. One area that remains understudied is whether many African Americans actually seek mental health treatment as a result of coping with witnessing police brutality. Despite this, African Americans may seek treatment for secondary problems such as depression or anxiety.

CLINICAL IMPLICATIONS

Based on the information discussed, it is important that we consider how racism and discrimination might impact our work with African American clients. For example, many clinicians may be reluctant to discuss issues of race relations with their clients. It is clear that racism and discrimination have a lasting impact on the mental health functioning of African Americans. However, despite many African Americans experiencing racism directly or indirectly, it is important to recognize that not all individuals will develop poor mental health outcomes (e.g., depression, anxiety, or race-related stress). Regardless, all mental health providers—both clinicians of African descent and those from other ethnic groups—must be prepared to explore and evaluate for race-related stress or other psychological symptoms that may result from experiencing a racist encounter.

In recent years, the literature has noted that indirect exposure to traumatic experiences through watching news media may be associated with increases in trauma-related symptoms (e.g., Bor et al., 2018; Galovski et al., 2016). Furthermore, some scholars noted that traumatic experiences tended to increase the risk of traumatization when those experiences involve an assault on the personhood or integrity of the victim, as is often the case with racist encounters such as police brutality (e.g., Bryant-Davis & Ocampo, 2005; Williams et al., 2018). For example, Galovski and colleagues (2016) found that following the killing in Ferguson, Black community members reported more symptoms of PTSD and depression compared to White community members. Despite the cultural trauma and historical racism experienced by many ethnic and racial groups in the United States, limited research exists on evidence-based practices for working with these populations to help address racial trauma (Williams et al., 2018). This is an area that will require much attention in the near future, particularly given the state of race-relations in the United States over the last 5 to 10 years. To help improve the field's understanding of this area, a recent special issue of *American Psychologist* focused on racial trauma (see Comas-Díaz et al., 2019). The special issue is focused on helping researchers and clinicians understand race-based stress and identify methods of culturally in-formed healing practices.

Recently, Williams and her colleagues (2018) have created a semi-structured assessment tool to increase our recognition of racial trauma. Although several measures exist to assess for PTSD (see Carlson, 2001; Carter et al., 2013; Williams et al., 2018), few provide sufficient prompts to assess for racial trauma. According to the authors, The UConn Racial/Ethnic Stress & Trauma Survey (UnRESTS; Williams et al., 2018) is intended to uncover forms of racism experienced by clients, which provide critical information to aid with case conceptualization and determining whether those racist experiences collectively are trau-matizing. Furthermore, the interview includes information regarding racial identity and a checklist to help determine whether the individu-al's racial trauma symptoms meet DSM criteria for PTSD. Refer to Williams, Metzger, Leins, and DeLapp (2018) for a complete descrip-tion. Although no current research exists on the clinical utility of the UnRESTS, it appears to offer a framework to assist researchers and clinicians with improving their understanding of racial trauma.

In addition to assessing for racial trauma, it is necessary for the field to help African American clients with healing from these discriminatory racial encounters (DREs) such as witnessing police violence or experi-encing racism. Anderson and Stevenson (2019) note that accumulating evidence indicates that the majority of African American youth and adults (approximately 90%) report some degree of DREs. However, most mental health providers have limited training on how to address DREs to improve the well-being of African American clients (Harrell, 2000). Although this is outside of the scope of this book, it is necessary to highlight areas that might be helpful clinically to promote healing. Given that racism is not eradicated, many people will continue to en-counter these experiences that could be detrimental to their psychological and physical health. According to Harrell (2000), mental health professionals can promote healing through identification, validation, and discussion of DREs. As discussed earlier, mental health providers often avoid discussions about racism or may be unsure how to address these with their clients. This could lead to pitfalls in the therapeutic relationship. Providers' biases may also "affect their ability to listen, understand, show empathy and respect, develop a strong therapeutic alliance, and engage in creative and relevant problem-solving" with African American clients (Harrell, 2000).

Some scholars have described psychological approaches to promote healing from race-based traumatic stress (e.g., Anderson, Jones et al., 2018; Anderson, McKenny et al., 2018; Harrell, 2000). At minimum, mental health providers should explore the use of different types of coping behaviors (e.g., engaging in social advocacy) and exploring ways to strengthen racial and ethnic identity (Harrell, 2000). More recently, Anderson and Stevenson (2019) have described how the Racial Encounter Coping Appraisal Socialization Theory (RECAST) may be a useful model to promote racial coping self-efficacy. RECAST is a "cognitive-behavioral intervention process that addresses emotional regulation and processing of DREs to reduce anxiety, promote self-efficacy and promote racial coping and agency" (Anderson & Stevenson, 2019). The RECAST method appears to be helpful to help individuals actively practice racial socialization, which may improve one's confidence and competence to deal with DREs. Building on the RECAST model, the Engaging, Managing, and Bonding through Race (EMBRace) intervention was developed, and emerging research with EMBRace shows promise for improving coping with DREs (For details, refer to Anderson & Stevenson, 2019, and Anderson, McKenny et al., 2018).

CONCLUSION

In general, there is a substantial amount of research on racism, discrimination, and police brutality that demonstrates the negative impacts on the psychological functioning of African Americans. Although these issues may not be directly discussed or addressed in therapy, it is clear that these may be concerns that contribute to African Americans' decisions to seek mental health services as a result of issues such as anxiety or depression. Currently, the literature is unclear regarding a diagnosis of PTSD as a result of experiencing a racist incident, but multiple scholars (Bryant-Davis & Ocampo, 2005; Williams et al., 2018) note that racism and discrimination may contribute to the higher rate of PTSD among African Americans. Furthermore, there is a clear need to better understand racial trauma. The field would particularly benefit from more data on the epidemiology of racial trauma, better tools for assessment and identification, and access to interventions to help African Americans cope with symptoms of race-related stress or racial trauma. In an ideal world, discrimination and various forms of racism would be nonexistent. Sadly, history has taught us that it is difficult to undo a system of oppression that was created with the formation of the United States.

3

THE FOUR A'S OF TREATMENT INITIATION

As a field, we have attempted to understand why many African Americans are reluctant to engage in seeking mental health treatment. According to decades of research, African Americans are one of the ethnic groups least likely to use mental health services (Snowden, 2001; Turner et al., 2016; USDHHS, 2001). Numerous studies have identified several barriers that impact mental health treatment use among diverse racial and ethnic groups (Snowden, 2001; Thompson, Bazile, & Akbar, 2004; USDHHS, 2001). This chapter discusses the Model of Treatment Initiation (MTI) and the research demonstrating the complexity of our understanding about the factors that contribute to African Americans avoiding or seeking mental health treatment.

Models of seeking mental health services have described several factors that contribute to individuals' decisions to seek treatment including attitudes toward professional help-seeking, awareness of when treatment-seeking is appropriate, mental health stigma, and financial costs. One of the most common models that have been applied to our understanding of mental health treatment use is the Theory of Planned Behavior (TPB) (Ajzen, 1991). The TPB has been used to demonstrate the impact of attitudes (i.e., how favorable or unfavorable a person views the behavior), subjective norms (i.e., societal views on performing or not performing the behavior), and perceived behavioral control (i.e., how easy or difficult the person views performing the behavior will be) on individuals' intentions to engage in a behavior such as seeking mental health treatment. Another model developed by Andersen (1995), the Behavioral Model of Health Service Use, has also been applied to describe how service use is a function of an individual's predisposing factors (e.g., demographics), enabling factors (e.g., community), and perceptions of need. Although these models are useful and have been supported by research, a perceived limitation of other help-seeking models prevents examining how multiple factors interact to influence therapy use. To better capture the complexity of how multiple variables cohesively contribute to help-seeking, especially for ethnic minorities, I have collaborated with other scholars to develop a conceptual model of help-seeking. The MTI helps to improve our understanding of the role of multiple factors that are associated with treatment-seeking (e.g., Turner et al., 2016; Turner, Malone, & Douglas, 2019). According to the MTI (Turner et al., 2016), four major areas influence treatment-seeking among ethnic minority groups: accessibility factors (structural variables that may influence an individual's ability to access treatment), availability factors (access to culturally competent services), appropriateness factors (how individuals view mental health problems as requiring treatment), and acceptability factors (variables such as stigma and cultural mistrust). Figure 3.1 highlights the Model of Treatment Initiation for African Americans.

ACCESSIBILITY FACTORS

One of the most consistent factors that influence mental health use among African Americans involves accessibility. Within the model of treatment initiation, accessibility factors may include affordability of services, availability of providers within the community, and other structural barriers. To better understand disparities in treatment-seeking, it is important to explore how accessibility factors contribute to underutilization of services. When considering help-seeking among African Americans in the United States, it is necessary to understand how accessibility factors influence the use of treatment.

Psychotherapy and mental health treatment can be costly despite adjusted fee schedules by providers or having insurance coverage. The literature has cited that affordability of services may impact some individuals' decisions to seek treatment (e.g. Snowden, 2001; USDHHS,

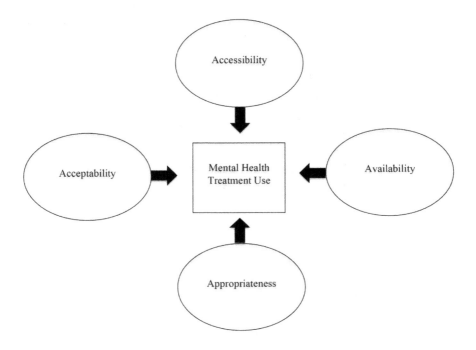

Figure 3.1. Model of Treatment Initiation for African Americans

Source: **Generated by the author.**

2001). However, financial constraints may impact utilization of treatment differently across demographic variables depending on the individuals' education or socioeconomic status. In general, what the literature indicates is that for many African Americans providing for their families may take precedence over paying for weekly therapy sessions. In my clinical work, I have found that some clients struggle to decide if they can commit to weekly therapy sessions. As a result, they may desire to attend therapy sessions less frequently given other financial responsibilities. These are important discussions that must occur with some African American clients at the beginning of treatment. Mental health providers should not assume that all African Americans are reluctant to attend regularly sessions solely based on financial need. However, if a client brings up concerns about the frequency of sessions, clinicians should be prepared to have an open conversation about possible options—which may include identifying a way to meet less frequently or to modify the fee schedule. In my opinion, financial considerations may play a role in early termination or treatment dropout for some African American clients. However, this is difficult to answer given that many clients stop coming to therapy without formally notifying their provider.

At times, the research on costs and mental health use has also been counterintuitive when we seek to explore how costs influence decisions to seek professional help for African Americans. It might be expected that when costs are high, clients are less likely to use professional services. However, the literature shows that for some African Americans cost may not be the biggest factor to consider. Some research shows that even when African Americans have insurance coverage, they are still less likely to seek services (Weisz & Weiss, 1991). In an experimental study conducted by Kugelmass (2016), results indicated that even when African American clients desire to seek treatment, they might also face challenges in receiving services due to discrimination by mental health professionals. Specifically, Kugelmass found racial and class differences in the frequency of appointments given to African Americans. The study noted that African American and working-class clients were less likely to receive an appointment when compared to Whites. Furthermore, the weekly cost associated with seeking treatment may be perceived as more costly (e.g., time commitment) than the benefits for some African Americans from high socioeconomic status backgrounds (Thompson, Bazile, & Akbar, 2004; Turner et al., 2016). Anecdotally, I have worked with clients across the socioeconomic spectrum and found that regardless of their background, the costs of treatment may factor into their decisions given other responsibilities that they have to consider regarding supporting their immediate or extended families.

When considering help-seeking among African Americans, it is also necessary to understand how structural factors influence the use of treatment. Within the MTI conceptualization, accessibility factors may include availability of providers within individuals' communities or access to transportation. This section is not intended to be exhaustive but to provide a brief discussion of some factors to consider when working with African Americans. In my experience working in the mental health professional for over a decade providing clinical services and conducting research, I have recognized that while some clients have serious financial considerations, others are more concerned about having a provider in proximity to their neighborhood. Availability of mental health clinics, psychiatric hospitals, or emergency room care may reduce access to mental health treatment. Often individuals delay treatment until the last minute because no provider is located in their community. This may also be a factor that contributes to more severe difficulties among this population because of challenges accessing care. Research indicates that African Americans are more likely to seek crisis intervention through emergency rooms (ER) to address their mental health concerns (Turner et al., 2016). One possible explanation for seeking ER treatment is because there is a lack of mental health providers in their area. As a result of seeking care through the ER, this often leads to possible difficulties with continued care. If African Americans are seen under crisis situations to manage psychological distress or mental health concerns, it may contribute to difficulties with establishing an ongoing relationship with a mental health provider. Although African American clients may be given a referral for outpatient mental health treatment, follow-up may be less likely due to numerous factors including cost, availability, or stigma.

Navigating the health-care system may pose another challenge to African Americans receiving mental health treatment. This can range from not having a clinic or behavioral health system in close proximity to not having a provider of color. As discussed later in the book, some African Americans may prefer a same-race mental health provider. This may be a significant barrier in terms of accessibility. It also highlights another issue related to cultural sensitivity within health care systems. In general, clients must incorporate attending therapy sessions into their weekly schedules, which might include work, school, or family obligations. For some African Americans, the ability to take off work to arrive at their therapy appointments may not be feasible. The inability to receive treatment in the evening (e.g., after 5:00 p.m.) may cause an additional barrier to seeking mental health treatment. In my experience working with families, African American parents often request appointments after school and/or work hours. Given limited availability during those times, it can be difficult to schedule appointments. After-school and evening hours are typically prime spots for most mental health providers. Therefore, African American clients or families who request those time slots tend to have a more difficult time getting treatment. This might also explain some of the findings in the Kugelmass (2016) study regarding African Americans having more difficulties receiving appointments compared to other ethnic groups.

Some African Americans are also hesitant to seek mental health treatment because of fear of mistreatment or hospitalization. As discussed in earlier chapters, the health-care system has historically engaged in unethical behavior that often resulted in unfair treatment, misdiagnosis, and over-hospitalization of African Americans. Research studies on the prevalence of African Americans in inpatient settings often report an overrepresentation compared to other ethnic and racial groups (Snowden & Holschuh, 1992). Due to rates of inpatient hospitalization, African American clients may not willingly seek mental health treatment due to fear.

Another important consideration related to accessibility is transportation concerns. This goes hand-in-hand with access to mental health systems. Transportation issues can range from using public transportation to not having a provider within driving distance. Obviously this issue is not specific to African Americans, as other ethnic groups may have similar concerns. However, depending on an individual's socioeconomic status, it may be a more significant barrier. For many low-income African Americans, proximity to mental health services within their communities may be especially important. They may rely on public transit (e.g., buses, subways) or ride-share as their primary mode of transportation. If health systems are not accessible by public transportation, it may reduce access to treatment. Furthermore, for individuals who use public transportation as a means to attend therapy, it may impact their arrival time. While working in inner-city Baltimore, there were occasional situations when a client or family would arrive a few minutes late or request to leave early due to bus or train schedules. These are important considerations that mental health providers need to recognize and help clients navigate. It is possible that when mental health providers are unable to be flexible regarding how the clients' transportation issues impact treatment, it could result in early termination or dropout.

Within the mental health care system, African Americans may also lack an awareness of expectations around treatment attendance. Some African American clients are reluctant to seek care because attending weekly therapy sessions may appear interruptive to their daily lives. One way to address this issue is to have an open dialogue with clients

about their expectations and your expectations regarding therapy attendance. Most African American clients expect that therapy will be weekly, but some may express a desire to come to treatment less often.
Research notes that some African American clients may endorse
psychological difficulties but are still less likely to perceive a need for
treatment. One study using a national sample of African American
adults found that although 47 percent reported having at least one
DSM diagnosis, only 5 percent perceived a need for treatment
(Williams, 2014). It is possible that despite having psychological difficulties or even a diagnosis, the expectations around attending weekly
therapy sessions may reduce the likelihood of seeking services. As a
mental health professional, it is your ethical responsibility to make modifications to treatment to ensure that the client receives appropriate
care. These modifications may have to take into consideration the flex-
ibility of treatment attendance. Attending therapy less frequently can
still benefit clients if they are willing to do the work. However, providers must be willing to actively monitor clinical progress and discuss any
challenges. Chapter 4 provides more detail on cultural competence and
addressing issues related to reducing barriers to treatment engagement.

AVAILABILITY FACTORS

For African American clients, concerns regarding the availability of providers contribute to their openness to seek mental health services. In
the literature on cultural competency, numerous variables have been
identified such as preferences for therapists of color and having respect
for one's cultural background (e.g., willingness of provider to discuss
issues around race). This section focuses primarily on the factors that
contribute to improving cultural competence. Consistent with the MTI,
availability factors include provider preferences such as having an
African American therapist or a provider who is culturally sensitive.
Having access to unbiased treatment is a significant factor in engaging
and retaining African American clients in treatment. African Americans
often report that they prefer working with someone who looks like
them. Studies often show that African American clients view same-race
providers as more credible, trustworthy, and unbiased (Turner, Malone,
& Douglas, 2019; Thompson & Alexander, 2006). Thompson and Alex-

ander (2006) found that African American clients assigned to racially matched therapists reported greater self-understanding, acceptance, and belief in the utility of treatment strategies than when they were assigned to White therapists. This example highlights that some African Americans perceive same-race providers as more culturally sensitive. In my experience, African American clients seek out same-race providers more frequently than cross-racial dyads. This may be due to their cultural values and their desire to feel connected.

Another factor to keep in mind when working with African American clients is that their racial or ethnic identities may shape their preferences regarding the selection of a provider. According to some scholars, individuals with a strong ethnic identity may prefer a provider of the same ethnic background. In a study conducted by Yasui, Hipwell, Stepp and Keenan (2015), the authors found that when comparing mental health service use among African American and European American families, ethnic identity was associated with decreased use of mental health services for African Americans. According to the authors, decreased use of mental health services may result due to therapy being inconsistent with their ethnic identities. Similar findings have also been found among African American adults (Obasi & Leong, 2009). Giving this research, it is important for mental health providers to keep in mind that diversity within the African American community may influence client-therapist interactions. In particular, those with a strong ethnic identity may have a more difficult time with developing rapport with a non-Black provider compared to African Americans that may adhere to more American values (i.e., acculturated).

Another potential issue that contributes to African American clients seeking treatment is the limited diversity within the mental health profession. Data indicates that the ethnic representation of African American mental health providers differs based on level of training. According to recent data from the American Psychological Association (2017d), 84 percent of psychologists identified as White and approximately 5 percent identified as African American. Data from the Substance Abuse and Mental Health Services Administration (SAMHSA, 2013) also report that across disciplines, racial and ethnic minorities account for 19 percent of psychiatrists, 5.1 percent of psychologists, 17.5 percent of social workers, 10.3 percent of counselors, and 7.8 percent of marriage and family therapists. Given the current diversity of the mental health profession, it is important that providers improve their ability to provide culturally sensitive treatment. African Americans may expect that their mental health providers feel comfortable discussing issues related to race, ethnicity, and culture (Turner, Malone, & Douglas, 2019). Research has demonstrated that African American clients who define themselves and their presenting problems using cultural constructs (i.e., race, ethnicity, and gender) tend to prefer racially or gender similar providers. If African American clients are working with a dissimilar race provider, it could reduce the likelihood that certain issues are discussed. This could be important with discussing possible race-related stress.

Although therapist matching might be important to some African American clients, research also indicates that not all African Americans prefer a same-race provider. Regardless of African Americans' preferences, it is necessary that professionals adhere to ethical standards when providing care. This includes having the knowledge, skills, and experience to work with clients from different ethnic or racial groups. Multicultural competence is important for several reasons including ethical responsibility. Key factors in multicultural competence include awareness of one's biases, understanding the worldview of the client, and providing appropriate intervention strategies and techniques. All of these factors are important when working with African American clients to address treatment engagement and success.

ACCEPTABILITY FACTORS

Acceptability factors are described as those that contribute to why an individual may desire to seek treatment or exhibit concerns about mistreatment by mental health providers. These factors may include mental illness stigma, cultural beliefs, fears about psychotherapy, and expectations about mental health treatment (e.g, Thompson et al., 2013; Yorke, Voisin, & Baptiste, 2016). Decades of research evidence have provided examples of variables that influence acceptability of mental health treatment among African Americans. The literature often highlights that among African Americans there is a large influence of family and cultural factors on their views about mental health. Furthermore, negative experiences within the mental health system may combine with those factors to heighten their reluctance to seek treatment either initially or in the future. Cultural views about mental health appear to be similar across the African diaspora (e.g. Boyd-Franklin, 2010; Yorke, Voisin, & Baptiste, 2016).

One of the most frequent factors related to acceptability is the focus on seeking support from the family to address psychological distress or mental health concerns. Research often documents the importance of social support across ethnic groups (Yorke, Voisin, & Baptiste, 2016). However, social support and the family system is often the preferred method of informal help-seeking for African Americans. Studies report that family members and friends often express ideas that formal mental health services are irrelevant and that mental health problems should be kept within the family (Turner et al., 2016). One study among a Caribbean immigrant population (i.e., Jamaican) found that strong social support was associated with decreased preferences for seeking formal mental health services (Yorke, Voisin, & Baptiste, 2016). The authors concluded that issues of mental health are considered a family issue and are not to be discussed with people outside of the immediate family. These views are held by many African Americans and often result in them not viewing mental health services as the first line of addressing psychological difficulties. Yorke and colleagues (2016) note that many Caribbean immigrants hold the belief that the family is responsible for an individual's problems and therefore mental health issues should be addressed within the family. Other scholars provide similar evidence among African American families (Boyd-Franklin, 2010; Horwitz, 1978).

Decades of injustice and oppression in the mental health system have also led to African Americans' decreased interest in mental health services (Turner, Malone, & Douglas, 2019). For example, one of the most significant incidents to date that has continued to plague treatment-seeking among African Americans was the Tuskegee syphilis study. In the Tuskegee syphilis study, African American airmen were enrolled in a study to treat the disease but never received the treatment as described. As a result of this historical event, many African Americans mistrust systems of care—including mental health. Cultural mistrust has been described as cultural paranoia or suspicion toward Whites or European Americans to protect against race-based persecution and discrimination (Grier & Cobbs, 1968; Whaley, 2001).

Cultural mistrust is evident in various communities of color and has implications for whether and how they interact with institutions of mental health, as well as how providers of these institutions respond to them as clients (Turner, Malone, & Douglas, 2019). For African Americans, cultural mistrust has significant implications on decisions to seek treatment. Studies have shown that higher levels of cultural mistrust among African Americans is associated with negative perceptions about mental health treatment, especially when services are provided by non-Black providers (e.g., Thompson et al., 2013; Whaley, 2001).

In regard to mental illness stigma, the research often finds that African Americans have more stigma toward treatment compared to other ethnic groups. Turner, Jensen-Doss, and Heffer (2015) reported that African Americans reported more mental health stigma toward services than White and Hispanic parents. This is generally consistent across multiple research studies (e.g., Belgrave & Allison, 2014; Turner et al., 2016). Research also describes how the term "psychotherapy" is often associated with stigma in the Black community (Thompson, Bazile, & Akbar, 2004). This may contribute to the lack of acceptability among African Americans, as they often view the use of mental health services as more appropriate for severe psychological disorders such as schizophrenia. This is captured by negative connotations that are associated with seeking treatment such as "being crazy" or "psycho." In a qualitative study conducted by Thompson and colleagues (2013), the authors reported that many African American mothers believed that seeking mental health treatment would further stigmatize their childen and therefore they avoided treatment to decrease these negative perceptions. One parent in the study reported, "Once you get in to see a psychiatrist, . . . they already got you labeled, that's the biggest rough part about any mental thing[—]you are labeled once you start" (Thompson et al., 2013, p. 10). Within the African diaspora, mental illness stigma appears to be a factor in treatment-seeking. Among Jamaican and Afro-Caribbean populations, stigma is associated with decreased use of professional mental health services (Yorke, Voisin, & Baptiste, 2016). Some purport that Caribbean immigrants may prefer to seek help from pastors or folk healers due to concerns about mental health practitioners (e.g., Nicolas, Jean-Jacques, & Wheatley, 2012; Yorke, Voisin, & Baptiste, 2016). As indicated in figure 3.1, stigma is only one possible factor that influences treatment. It is important to recognize that individual differences exist within the African American community and not every African American will display stigma toward treatment.

APPROPRIATENESS FACTORS

Finally, African Americans' use of services is associated with how they perceive their concerns should be addressed with mental health treatment or other methods of healing. Due to the large percentage of African Americans who have strong religious or spiritual beliefs, many may prefer to cope with mental health issues by not seeking professional mental care. Research indicates that prayer is an important coping strategy for many African Americans, especially those with lower incomes, females, and older adults over age 55 (Belgrave & Allison, 2014). Furthermore, data show that a high percentage of African Americans regularly attend church services or seek pastoral counseling to address their difficulties that could otherwise benefit from mental health services (Boyd-Franklin, 2010; Boyd-Franklin & Lockwood, 1999).

Spirituality and religion may also serve as a protective factor that helps to reduce the burden of mental health concerns. Some research demonstrates that African Americans who have strong religious beliefs or engage in religious practices (e.g., prayer) are less likely to suffer from difficulties. This may possibly help explain why many individuals use religious coping as their go-to strategy. When African American clients seek treatment, it is important for providers to explore the importance of these factors on the individual's functioning and coping.

CONCLUSION

Currently, the mental health literature highlights numerous barriers that impact the use of mental health treatment among African Americans. Discrimination and mistreatment by the profession continues to be a concern that prevents many African Americans from accessing mental health care. Based on several studies, perceived discrimination may be one of the most significant factors that influence treatment initiation (e.g., Belgrave & Allison, 2014; Kugelmass, 2016). Furthermore, cultural sensitivity or lack thereof may influence early termination among this population. As described in the MTI, cultural values and beliefs play an important role on African Americans' decisions to seek mental health treatment. Turner and colleagues (2016) note research on the importance of family connectedness and keeping information within the family as a barrier. To improve the use of mental health services among this group, the field needs to continue identifying ways to change perceptions about treatment and improve clinicians' ability to engage in practice with African American clients.

4

CLINICAL PRACTICE WITH AFRICAN AMERICAN CLIENTS

Cultural competency has been defined as providing services to a population while incorporating knowledge of the client's background and applying clinical skills in a culturally sensitive manner (e.g., Chu et al., 2016; Sue, 2006). As discussed throughout this book, culturally sensitive treatment influences client-therapist interactions and therapeutic effectiveness. Culturally competent therapists are aware of and sensitive to their own cultural heritage and are comfortable with the differences that may exist across the client-therapist dyad (Sue, 2006; Sue, Gallardo, & Neville, 2013). The goal of this chapter is to overview the important aspects of cultural competency, provide a framework for understanding the role of culture and ethnicity in the treatment process, and discuss the research on competency and treatment with African American clients.

CULTURAL COMPETENCE FRAMEWORK

As the fields of counseling and psychotherapy have changed over the years, many have recognized the importance of integrating one's cultural background into the treatment process. When providers are culturally sensitive, they hold specific knowledge about diverse racial and ethnic minority groups, understand the generic characteristics of providing therapy, and possess the skills and abilities to generate a wide

variety of verbal and nonverbal responses within the counseling relationship (Sue, 2006; Sue et al., 2009). What does it mean to be culturally competent? Is it possible to reach a threshold of "competence" when
working with diverse groups of clients? Historically the field has defined cultural competency as including (1) cultural awareness and beliefs, (2) cultural knowledge, and (3) cultural skills. Cultural awareness
and beliefs focus on the providers' self-awareness regarding the attitudes and beliefs, biases, and assumptions with respect to their own
culture of origin (e.g., Arredondo, 1999; Sue, 2006; Sue, Gallardo, &
Neville, 2013). Mental health providers who are competent in cultural
knowledge "possess knowledge and understanding about how oppression, racism, discrimination, and stereotyping affect them personally
and their work" (Arredondo, 1999, p. 103). Arredondo (1999) stresses
that this applies to all ethnic groups, but White+ counselors should also
recognize how direct or indirect privilege influence their client-therapist relationship. Finally, cultural skills focus on working within a multicultural perspective and being responsible for educating clients to the
process of therapy including discussing goals, expectations, and providers' theoretical orientation to treatment (e.g., Arredondo, 1999; Turner,
Malone, & Douglas, 2019).

More recently, some scholars have provided a conceptual framework
to describe why "cultural competency" is important (e.g., Chu et al.,
2016). The first principle in the model is creating a contextual match
with the client's external realities. In my opinion, many African
American clients often feel that their therapists do not understand their
perspective. Either indirectly or directly, those therapists do not recognize how contextual factors within the environment may be causing
their clients psychological distress. To improve cultural competency
with African Americans, attention must be given to addressing and
understanding how these factors impact the therapeutic relationship
and clinical outcomes. This potential mismatch between understanding
the client's environment and the therapist's perceptions of the client
may lead to an inaccurate diagnosis and subsequently less effective
intervention. Chapter 5 discusses more details about how understanding cultural factors might help therapists to connect with clients and better understand how contextual factors influence the
therapeutic relationship.

The second principle of cultural competency is creating an experiential match in the microsystem. This involves ensuring that the provider understands how the client's family and community (e.g., school, church) have a direct influence on the individual. To address experiential match, research shows how connecting clients with a same-race therapist enhances the therapeutic environment. Research concludes that ethnic matching between therapists and clients helps improve the client's perceptions of the therapist as credible, trustworthy, and less biased (Chu et al., 2016). However, ethnic matching does not ensure cultural competence. As discussed in chapter 3, some African American clients may not have a preference to be matched with an African American mental health provider. Therefore, it is important to establish at the outset of treatment whether a client has a strong preference toward a same-race provider. In circumstances where there is a strong preference for a same-race provider, a mismatch in the therapeutic environment may lead to barriers with engaging the client in treatment.

The third principle of cultural competency is creating an environment where the client feels understood and empowered. Cultural humility involves a process of self-reflection and awareness. Cultural humility allows the therapist to be open to the client's beliefs, values, and worldview as opposed to viewing the therapist's beliefs and values as superior (Bernal & Adames, 2017; Gallardo, 2013). When the clients' cultural beliefs are significantly different from their mental health providers, rapport and treatment success may be affected (Sue, 1998). Although we all have biases, it is important for therapists to not let those biases impact their relationship with their clients. It is the responsibility of mental health providers to be open to the moment, to ask the right questions, and to gather the information using methods that are inclusive and sensitive to the clients' culture. Anecdotally, I have worked with clients who come to therapy to discuss concerns and who occasionally have reported past experiences with other providers in which they felt as if the provider was just there to "collect a paycheck." This often results in a therapeutic environment that is toxic and not supportive. According to Chu and colleagues (2016), engaging in cultural humility or empathy allows mental health providers to effectively communicate their understanding of the client's background.

GENERAL GUIDELINES FOR MULTICULTURAL PRACTICE

Guidelines for psychologists and other mental health professionals often identify principles for practicing with diverse groups by providing an overview of the important skills that clinicians should demonstrate to be ethical and effective in their work. Some of the earliest guidelines put forth by the American Psychological Association (APA) for working with culturally and ethnically diverse populations were developed by the APA Task Force on the Delivery of Services to Ethnic Minority Populations in 1988 (APA, 2002). The goal of these guidelines was primarily to assist psychologists with improving the quality of services provided to individuals from diverse ethnic and cultural groups. These guidelines were known as the Guidelines for Providers of Psychological Services to Ethnic, Linguistic, and Culturally Diverse Populations. They were originally published in 1991 by the APA Office of Minority Affairs and later disseminated in *American Psychologist*. These guidelines established nine principles for psychologists that covered broad areas including educating the client about the process and limits of confidentiality, psychologists' competence related to the populations they serve, reducing prejudice and biases in interactions with clients, respecting clients' beliefs (e.g., religious), and addressing cultural and sociopolitical factors. Please refer to APA (2002) for the complete guidelines.

In 2002, the American Psychological Association approved a document (*Guidelines on Multicultural Education, Training, Research, Practice, and Organizational Change for Psychologists*) that shaped the field's practices toward addressing the needs of a growing diverse society (APA, 2002; 2003). In collaboration with many experts within the field of psychology, the guidelines sought to address the needs of individuals, children, and families from diverse groups. The 2002 Multicultural Guidelines (APA, 2002; 2003) provided six principles to address cultural competence: knowledge of self with a cultural heritage and varying social identities and knowledge of other cultures. For approximately 10 years, these guidelines were instrumental in influencing how psychologists engaged in psychological practice with individuals from culturally and ethnically diverse groups. However, it was noted that these guidelines were developed with a narrow focus that strongly leaned toward how providers integrate race/ethnicity into their work.

Given these potential limitations and the increasing diversity within the United States it became more important to integrate an innovative perspective when considering the factors that influence psychological practice, education, and training.

Current Perspectives on Multicultural Practice

When APA published the 2002 Multicultural Guidelines, the expectation was that these guidelines for psychological practice would be updated within 10 years. In 2015, a task force was created to revise and update the original multicultural guidelines. In 2017, the APA adopted the new multicultural guidelines (*Multicultural Guidelines: An Ecological Approach to Context, Identity, and Intersectionality*) as APA policy. These guidelines provide 10 principles that psychologist should address when providing multiculturally competent psychological services. In contrast to the 2002 guidelines, the 2017 version includes perspectives from other fields outside of psychology such as psychiatry and social work (see APA, 2017c for a complete discussion).

The 2017 APA *Multicultural Guidelines* seek to primarily address identity and self-definitions, recognition by psychologists of communication when working with diverse populations, awareness of the social environment, the role of power and privilege, the importance of conducting culturally appropriate research, and how to apply a strength-based approach. Although all of these concepts may not be appropriate when working with African American clients, the guidelines are helpful for understanding what roles behavioral health providers (e.g., psychologists and therapists) must consider when providing care to diverse populations.

The 2017 *Multicultural Guidelines* represent advances in how we conceptualize psychological practice within a multicultural society. As noted in the guidelines, "we must consider diversity and multicultural practice within professional psychology at a different time period" (APA, 2017c, p. 6). This is acknowledged by the guidelines being inclusive of intersecting identities. In contrast to the narrow focus of the original guidelines, the 2017 version uses a broader scope to capture multiculturalism within the context of a global society. According to the guidelines, this approach reflects current perspectives on "the influence of contextual factors and intersectionality among and between reference group identities, including culture, language, gender, race, ethnicity, ability status, sexual orientation, age, gender identity, socioeconomic status, religion, spirituality, immigration status, education, and employment, among other variables" (APA, 2017c). Furthermore, the 2017 guidelines apply an ecological conceptualization (see figure 4.1). The benefits of applying an ecological model to cultural competence allow for providers to understand the bidirectional nature of interpersonal interactions, as well as how the larger society influences the clients' actions, experiences, and perceptions toward psychological services. Refer to the APA *Multicultural Guidelines* (APA, 2017c) for a more complete description of the Layered Ecological Model.

The subsequent scenario discusses some of the specific areas of the *Multicultural Guidelines* that may be most pertinent when working with African Americans. For example, the guidelines are useful to explore the dynamics of power and privilege in the therapy relationship when providing services to African American clients (see Guideline 5). According to the *Multicultural Guidelines* (APA, 2017c), power and privilege can be manifested through the experiences of the client in session. Therefore, psychologists and providers should explore how these factors influence their relationships with clients.

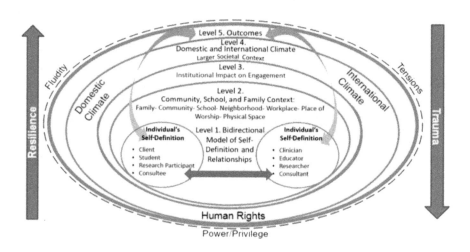

Figure 4.1. Layered Ecological Model of the Multicultural Guidelines

Source: American Psychological Association (2017c). Published with permission.

Case Vignette[1]: Kimberly is an eight-year-old African American girl who is referred for treatment of ADHD [attention deficit hyperactivity disorder] by her parents. The family reported to their provider that they identify as African American and occasionally feel that they are mistreated due to their race. Kimberly's mother stated that she and her husband are very spiritual and inquired if their provider believed in God. The parents also expressed that they each identify with different religions. In the initial session, the provider was welcoming to the family but was reluctant to disclose [his or her] religious beliefs to the family. However, the provider worked to explore the family's ethnic identity and importance of religion. Given the avoidance of certain topics by the provider (e.g., not discussing past perceptions of mistreatment and provider's religious affiliation), the family did not return to the follow-up appointment.

The scenario above highlights several important considerations when working with African American clients. Although this discussion is not intended to be exhaustive, it provides some insights to keep in mind. First, applying the "Layered Ecological Model of the Multicultural Guidelines" (see figure 4.1), this example stresses Level 3, "Institutional Impact on Engagement," demonstrating how the client-therapist experiences within their communities have a bidirectional influence on relationships in the counseling session. The provider's avoidance of addressing the family's mistreatment had a negative influence on the decision of the family to continue treatment. Although unknown from the description, it is possible that the therapeutic alliance could have been strengthened if the provider was more direct in exploring the client's experience with potential racism. Secondly, several of the *Multicultural Guidelines* were referenced (i.e., see Guidelines 4, 5, and 10). For example, the provider neglected to explore the role of the family's social and physical environment on their functioning (Guideline 4). How does this shape their perceptions of mental health treatment or of the providers? How do their religious beliefs influence their values on parenting? Those are some questions that might be important to explore with the family. Furthermore, the provider appeared to lack insight into how power, privilege, and/or oppression may influence treatment progress (Guideline 5). Again, despite the limited details in the scenario, it is possible that the family perceived the provider (regardless of race) as perpetrating further oppression by not acknowledging historical discrimination. Finally, the provider acknowledged the family's cultural beliefs and values by exploring ethnic identity and religion. This information could be helpful to further engage the family and explore interventions that build on the strengths of the family (Guideline 10).

RESEARCH AND TREATMENT OUTCOMES

Mental health professionals have an ethical responsibility to facilitate psychological improvement in all clients regardless of their ethnicity (Arredondo & Toporek, 2004; Smith & Trimble, 2016). As noted earlier, many scholars have described aspects of multicultural competence (MC) including awareness, knowledge, and beliefs (Smith & Trimble, 2016; Sue, Arredondo, & McDavis, 1992). According to Smith and Trimble (2016), despite the field's understanding of the importance of cultural competency, there is limited data on how multicultural competency affects clients' perspectives and outcomes in therapy. In a meta-analysis on cultural competence and therapy outcomes, the researchers analyzed data from 16 studies (Smith & Trimble, 2016). The authors reported that across the studies, the strength of the association between therapists' competence and clients' perceptions ranged from weak to strong (correlations ranged from –0.25 to 0.83). In my interpretation of the findings, it appears that part of the reason for the large discrepancy across studies is due to therapists' versus clients' ratings of multicultural competence. When therapists rated their own levels of MC it was often less associated with positive client outcomes. It seems that therapists' perceptions of their competence does not always translate into how their clients experience their interactions during assessment and/or treatment. However, one should not discount the significance of cultural competence in treatment despite the limited empirical data available. Therapists' MC may not matter much if we rely on therapists' judgments, but therapists' MC may be critical from the perspective of the client (Smith & Trimble, 2016; Worthington, Soth-McNett, & Moreno, 2007). According to Smith & Trimble (2016), primary data is preferable to unsupported rhetoric. The research on MC in actual practice appears to be lacking, given that less than 20 studies exist over the course of several decades. However, the current evidence demonstrates positive associations between MC and the clients' experiences in therapy (Jones, Huey, & Rubenson, 2018; Smith & Trimble, 2016; Worthington, Soth-McNett, & Moreno, 2007).

Smith and Trimble (2016) note that research indicates that MC is positively related to several outcomes including clients' perceptions of therapists' trustworthiness and expertness (r = 0.50), clients' decisions to participate or terminate treatment (r = 0.26), and clients' improvement in treatment (r = 0.16). Across studies, only a small portion of clients' improvement is due to MC, as expected, given the bulk of research suggests that other variables such as the therapeutic relationship have a stronger influence on outcomes (Smith & Trimble, 2016; Webb, DeRubeis, & Barber, 2010), notwithstanding the following limitations: more than half of the studies used clients from university research studies, the majority of participants were either African American or Latino, few examined therapy changes over an extended time period, and the studies sample sizes were often less than 200 participants. More recent research has sought to address weaknesses by examining MC with actual clients (Owen et al., 2011; Smith & Trimble, 2016).

Approximately 10 years ago, Worthington, Soth-McNett, and Moreno (2007) conducted a content analysis of empirical studies addressing multicultural competence involving the four major ethnic minority groups: Native American/Alaskan Native, African American, Asian American, and Hispanic/Latino. Despite the theoretical emphasis on the need for cultural competence, some (Weinrach & Thomas, 2004) speculate that there is no evidence that providers that are skilled in working with diverse populations are better mental health providers than those who lack cultural competence. In their article, Worthington and colleagues (2007) analyzed data from 81 studies examining the influence of cultural competency on several outcomes (e.g., treatment satisfaction, attrition, and provider's effectiveness). In general, they found that being multiculturally competent is associated with more positive outcomes. For example, one study found that clients assigned to counselors who completed cultural sensitivity training return for more sessions than did clients assigned to counselors in the control condition (Wade & Bernstein, 1991). However, some caveats were noted such as the majority of the research involved self-report measures, European Americans/Whites represented the largest percentage of participants (over 60%), and the majority of the studies used convenience samples or pseudo-clients (82.4%).

Research consistently reports that African Americans are less likely to seek treatment and often prematurely end services (Constantine, 2007; Jones, Huey, & Rubenson 2018; Turner et al., 2016). Factors that contribute to disparities may include experiences of poverty, incarceration, and racism (Jones, Huey, & Rubenson, 2018). Furthermore, as noted earlier in the text, factors such as accessibility, therapists' cultural competence, and cultural mistrust also contribute to clients' reluctance to seek treatment. In general, advocates and researchers who promote cultural competence continue to grapple with determining the best way to broaden providers' awareness and attention to cultural differences in treatment while minimizing the likelihood of providers' inadvertently stereotyping clients or making treatment recommendations based solely on the client's race/ethnicity (Jones, Huey, & Rubenson, 2018). It is important to consider that cultural competence in practice entails the recognition of the client's diversity including their gender identity, age, sexual orientation/identity, socioeconomic status, ability status, religious and spiritual beliefs, national origin, immigration status, level of acculturation, educational level, and historical life experiences. When working with African American clients, mental health providers should also consider these factors during assessment and treatment.

One important consideration related to cross-racial dyads and cultural competence is centered on discussions around race and racial issues for African American clients. Certain therapists who are either ambivalent about or opposed to the notion that a cross-cultural approach is important in the counseling relationship may ascribe to what is referred to as a universalistic approach in their work with clients of color (Thompson & Jenal, 1994). These providers tend to stress attributes that are common among all people rather than stressing distinguishing characteristics of a specific racial group despite the client's race and ethnicity or culture (Thompson & Jenal, 1994). This is problematic for several reasons. The main reason being that it is not consistent with the field's general emphasis on integrating the importance of the clients' ethnicity and cultural values. Thompson and Jenal (1994) state that when African American clients are assigned to work with non-Black therapists (such as European American/White) that adhere to a color-blind perspective and avoid attending to race or racial issues, many

African American clients may perceive these providers as denying the impact of racial inequalities on their lives.

The work of Thompson and Jenal (1994) highlights the significance of racial conversations on cultural competence with this population. In their study, the authors selected 24 universal content condition videotapes of four counselors (two White, two Black) conducting quasi-counseling sessions with Black female college students. Sessions reflected the universal content condition, whereby counselors were instructed to address aspects of the participants' concern that could relate to others regardless of race. For example, if the participant commented that she "felt isolated on campus, as a black student," the counselor would reflect a statement such as "so, as a student on campus you have felt isolated and alone." Results indicated that African American clients appeared frustrated and exasperated when race was avoided in therapy. In my opinion, it seems that one of the challenges when working with African American clients that may result in early termination is a lack of comfort working with White therapists due to perceptions that their experiences within the context of American society may not be fully understood. This supports a strong case for more providers of African descent entering the profession and a need for White providers to directly address issues of racial mismatch in treatment.

Another important emphasis related to cultural competence is the use of culturally sensitive interventions. Some note that culturally sensitive interventions are necessary to increase engagement among African Americans in therapy to improve outcomes (Bernal & Adames, 2017; Jones, Huey, & Rubenson, 2018; Turner et al., 2016). One of the challenges with examining evidence-based treatments for African Americans is that few randomized controlled trials (RCTs) exist with this population. However, Jones, Huey, and Rubenson (2018) note that evidence-based treatments for African American youth and adults exist and studies generally support their effectiveness. Some may question whether evidence-based treatments that are developed and tested are equally effective with African Americans. Research on youth-focused treatments generally finds that there are no reliable differences in outcomes (Jones, Huey, & Rubenson, 2018). However, one limitation of these studies is that treatment outcomes for European American youth were compared with ethnic minority youth (e.g., Latino, Asian American), as opposed to specifically examining the treatment with

African American youth. Similarly, studies often find no significant differences in outcomes among African American adults (Jones, Huey, & Rubenson, 2018). Given the evidence on treatment disparities and early termination among African American clients, some may question how psychotherapy might be improved for this population.

Evidence exists supporting the use of evidence-based treatments with African Americans, but the findings are often correlational and lack studies demonstrating treatment outcomes specifically targeting this population (Jones, Huey, & Rubenson, 2018). Culturally adapted treatments that involve systematically modifying the intervention to make it more congruent with values, beliefs, and practices of African Americans may be particularly useful (Jones, Huey, & Rubenson, 2018). In general, the literature notes the following key themes that are important to consider when working with African Americans: openness to addressing racism and issues surrounding race, fostering positive racial/ethnic identity, and incorporating the clients' spiritual and religious values (Boyd-Franklin, 2010; Jones, Huey, & Rubenson, 2018; Turner, Malone, & Douglas, 2019). Meta-analysis typically demonstrates that interventions targeting African Americans yield small-to-medium effect sizes, which is comparable to culturally adapted treatments used with other ethnic groups (Jones, Huey, & Rubenson, 2018). When examining culturally adapted treatments among African Americans, limited studies exist. Jones, Huey, and Rubenson (2018) note that despite the lack of evidence, culturally adapted treatments may be beneficial relative to standard treatment approaches.

Regarding culturally adapted interventions with African Americans, two common methods exist regarding cultural tailoring. In a recent review, the authors report that Afrocentric models and client-therapist ethnic matching are often used to address cultural competence when working with African Americans (Jones, Huey, & Rubenson, 2018). Some of the concerns with the research on Afrocentric intervention approaches include that the treatments are (1) often group based, (2) gender specific, and (3) limited to African American heritage (Jones, Huey, & Rubenson, 2018). It appears that the literature is almost void of examining the treatment efficacy and effectiveness with populations such as African, Afro-Caribbean, and Haitian. In regard to ethnic matching, the literature is mixed regarding the benefits of African American clients working with African American mental health providers. Some studies report that ethnic matching is associated with improved treatment outcomes (e.g., reduced symptoms) and others find that matching is not always beneficial for African American clients (Constantine, 2007; Korchin 1980; Jones, Huey, & Rubenson, 2018; Webb, 2008). According to Jones, Huey, and Rubenson (2018), ethnic matching may increase client-therapist rapport and lead to discussions of more vulnerable content that they may not share with non-Black providers due to cultural mistrust, experiences of discrimination, or stereotype threat.

Given the current knowledge base on culturally adapted interventions with African Americans, we must engage in more and better research to clarify the benefits of these interventions. Specifically, we need to understand what factors contribute to treatment success and for which group characteristics (e.g., strong racial/ethnic identity). Some research demonstrates that African American clients perceive culturally adapted treatments as less credible (Webb, 2008; 2009). Additionally, some note that standard empirically supported treatments may be more effective for less acculturated African Americans (Jones, Huey, & Rubenson, 2018). Webb (2008) notes that "culturally specific treatments may be more effective at engaging African Americans in treatment and reducing drop-out, but the benefits may be short lived and decline over time." One concern about the use of cultural adaptations is that by modifying the intervention, the core components are diluted, which results in inefficiencies in treatment implementation (Bernal & Adames, 2017; Jones, Huey, & Rubenson, 2018).

FUTURE DIRECTIONS IN CULTURAL SENSITIVITY WITH AFRICAN AMERICANS

The importance of cultural competency is becoming more important as the diversity of the Untied States continues to shift. It is particularly necessary that providers recognize that many African American clients have expectations for therapists to discuss sensitive cultural issues and be open to navigating issues around race during treatment. With regard to African Americans, more work needs to be done to establish what aspects are particularly important when working with this population. As discussed in chapter 5, this is especially important for non-U.S.-born

African Americans. Some scholars have stated that "culture is only one relevant factor in providing effective mental health treatment and that depending on the circumstances, other aspects of a client may be more influential" (Sue et al., 2009). Sue and colleagues (2009) acknowledge that cultural competence should be approached from multiple levels of analysis: provider and treatment level, agency or institutional level (e.g., the operations of a mental health agency), and systems level (e.g., systems of care in a community).

In terms of culturally sensitive interventions, there remains limited research that identifies approaches that have been developed or tailored specifically for African Americans. Much of the literature on treatment efficacy often does not examine the acceptability of treatments delivered to specific population groups such as African Americans (Bernal & Adames, 2017). This has led to some criticism regarding testing interventions with ethnic groups that were developed with majority White samples. According to Bernal and Adames (2017), "utilizing interventions without the awareness of culture and context, psychologists may risk imposing assumptions, concepts, and practices on ethnocultural groups where they do not fit." When working with African Americans, it can be more challenging given within-group differences. Although there are important values and beliefs that should be considered, it is important for mental health professionals to ascertain how these values individually apply when they are providing psychological services to individuals or families.

Bernal and Adames (2017) offer numerous recommendations for improving cultural competence:

- Use a conceptual adaptation framework to identify key treatment elements and document all necessary adaptations.
- Evaluate treatment outcomes of the culturally adapted intervention.
- Examine the fidelity of the treatment intervention compared to the standard/original treatment.
- Reevaluate outcomes of the refined adapted evidence-based treatment.
- Involve the target population in the process of developing the content of the intervention.
- Consult with treatment providers who have expertise and knowledge working with the target population.

- Conduct a pilot study on the acceptability and feasibility of the adapted intervention.
- Identify specific details, themes, and barriers to delivery of the intervention. (p. 18)

Jones, Huey, and Rubenson (2018) also identify several methods to consider to advance practice with African American clients: (1) base cultural adaptations on culturally salient risks and strengths, (2) use reverse engineering to modify treatment interventions, and (3) integrate the use of "generic" strategies with implicit cultural elements. For more details, refer to Jones, Huey, and Rubenson (2018). The following section briefly elaborates on these considerations.

Jones, Huey, and Rubenson (2018) identify the importance of adapting treatments for African Americans by incorporating salient risks and strengths. This is consistent with the notion of applying an Afrocentric perspective with this population. Some work demonstrating the significance of culturally sensitive treatments have found positive outcomes (e.g., Davis et al., 2009; Jones, Huey, & Rubenson, 2018; Kaslow et al., 2010). For example, scholars have designed and evaluated the use of *nia* (a Swahili word defined as "purpose")—a culturally informed psychoeducation intervention—on treating suicidal behavior among African American women (Davis et al., 2009; Kaslow et al., 2010). The nia intervention uses African proverbs, attends to African American heroines and role models, and emphasizes culturally relevant coping strategies (spirituality, religious involvement) to enhance self-awareness and connection (Davis et al., 2009). The intervention addresses coping strategies and teaches African American women skills to change power imbalances in their relationships (Davis et al., 2009; Jones, Huey, & Rubenson, 2018). In general, the findings suggest that the psychoeducation intervention is effective for reducing suicidal ideation and symptoms of depression compared to treatment as usual (Davis et al., 2009; Kaslow et al., 2010).

Another method to improve cultural competence is through the development of interventions that use reverse engineering. According to Jones, Huey, & Rubenson (2018), to improve cultural competence, research could (a) dismantle interventions and identify specific components that are optimal for African Americans, (b) include those cultural components in exiting interventions, and (c) evaluate if those culturally modified interventions improve outcomes compared to usual standards of care. One study using Multidimensional Family Therapy consisting of culturally relevant factors found that the intervention improved treatment engagement among African American youth (Jackson-Gilfort et al., 2001). One caveat should be noted when developing or evaluating culturally specific interventions: some African American clients may perceive providers as being biased or overgeneralizing values based on their ethnicity. Jones, Huey, and Rubenson (2018) hypothesize that these interactions in psychotherapy may result in clients becoming angry or agitated. This is consistent with the findings of experiential research on multicultural competence (e.g., Thompson & Jenal, 1994).

Finally, Jones, Huey, and Rubenson (2018) recommend using generic strategies such as empathy building and role induction as "add-on" components to standard interventions. Role induction may specifically be useful with African American clients because it helps providers strengthen the client-therapist relationship by providing psychoeducation on the treatment process (Jones, Huey, & Rubenson, 2018). Scholars have reported that applying role induction as a component of treatment has demonstrated effectiveness with African Americans (e.g., Jones, Huey, & Rubenson, 2018; Katz et al., 2004). For example, Katz and colleagues (2004) reported that individuals who received a role induction intervention were more likely to attend treatment and less likely to engage in dropout compared to a treatment-as-usual group. This appears to show promise with respect to using role induction as an add-on treatment with this population.

CONCLUSION

Cultural competence is a necessary aspect of ethical practice. Overall, the field of psychological practice has improved over time to be more sensitive to recognizing and fostering the integration of ethnic and cultural issues in multicultural research and practice. However, we still have work to do with respect to understanding within-group variability in practice with African American populations. As discussed, evidence-based assessment and interventions are important but the evidence is mixed regarding use with African Americans. It is clear that more is desired to better understand how to improve services with this population.

NOTE

1. All names are pseudonyms and all identifying factors have been removed to ensure anonymity.

5

AFRICAN AMERICAN VALUES

Working with African Americans in clinical practice requires that clinicians check themselves at the outset of treatment to avoid allowing stereotypes to hinder their ability to establish rapport. Many clients may avoid treatment due to their perceptions that mental health providers are not sensitive to their individual needs. As discussed in chapter 3, one frequent barrier to treatment is the lack of providers' cultural sensitivity. Scholars have also mentioned that African American clients have difficulties with feeling comfortable working with non-Black providers because of concerns about discussing issues around race and discrimination (e.g., Arredondo & Toporek, 2004; Chen, Kakkad, & Balzano, 2008; Turner, Malone, & Douglas, 2019). The goal of this chapter is to discuss broad cultural values that are important to consider when working with African American clients. It is critical that providers recognize that African Americans may adhere to these values across a spectrum. Therefore, it is necessary to not overgeneralize these variables. We must consider that not all African Americans have the same belief systems nor do they all strongly identify with their ethnic or racial group (e.g., Boyd-Franklin, 2003; Morris, 2001).

Many mental health providers are trained to provide therapy within a Eurocentric or Western perspective. Lowy (1995) describes Eurocentrism as incorporating values of Europe and Europeans to develop an ideology about racial, religious, cultural, or ethnic supremacy over other groups of people. According to Morris (2001), Eurocentric values involve an emphasis on individuality, authoritativeness, nuclear family structure, and competitiveness. Morris (2001) also notes that Western-ized or Eurocentric theoretical perspectives are "inadequate in explain-ing the psychological mindset of most African Americans." Consistent with approaching therapy from the lens of cultural sensitivity, it is nec-essary to explore how cultural values and beliefs contribute to an indi-vidual's functioning and resiliency. To address this issue, applying African-Centered Psychology is beneficial.

Some scholars (Baldwin, 1986) have a debated whether African-Centered or Black Psychology should capture the entire African experi-ence (both U.S. and non-U.S. born) or only focus on U.S.-born African Americans. Most of the definitions are consistent with those of Wade Nobles, who defined Black Psychology in terms of how it applies to the African experience—rooted in the nature of Black culture, which is based on indigenous philosophical assumptions of Africa—and in gen-eral to African Americans (Baldwin, 1986; Belgrave & Allison, 2014). African Americans are strongly influenced by their African heritage and culture (Willis, 1989). Therefore, it is imperative that mental health providers incorporate aspects of their cultural identity into treatment. Unfortunately, most mental health training programs do not offer train-ing in Black Psychology to their students.

The African-Centered perspective or Afrocentric worldview derives from a perspective that conceptualizes the lives of people of African ancestry in terms of African history, culture, and philosophy (Randolph & Banks, 1993). Throughout this book, Africentric and Afrocentric per-spectives are used interchangeably. According to Grills (2004), African Psychology consists of African values, ways of accessing knowledge, ways of defining reality, ways of governing and interpreting behaviors, and social relations in designing environments to sustain healthy, adap-tive functioning among people of African descent. Numerous scholars and Black psychologists have described values consistent with an Afro-centric perspective (e.g., key figures Wade Nobles, Na'im Akbar, Asa Hilliard, and Linda James Myers). Africentric values may include em-phasis on the group and relationships, democratic orientation, extended family structure, interdependence or communalism, social time phe-nomenon, spirituality, thriving under harmony or integration of all as-pects of one's life, and verbal tradition (e.g., Belgrave & Allison, 2014; Boyd-Franklin, 2003; Morris, 2001).

Many African Americans may prematurely terminate therapy due to a mismatch in therapist-client expectations about treatment. Morris (2001) claims that when therapists are "operating in the dark" they can make faulty assumptions that lead to inaccurate diagnosis and the creation of unsuccessful treatment plans. When approaching therapy from a Eurocentric perspective, it may result in the therapist not actively integrating the clients' values into treatment. This may result in the provider "operating in the dark" and discounting the influence of African value systems within the context of therapy, as well as the clients' functioning.

Working with African Americans clients requires that the provider intentionally explore the client's racial and ethnic identity. Not all African Americans come from the same cultural mind-set, not all African Americans have the same worldviews, and not all African Americans are at the same stage of identity development (Morris, 2001). Some have questioned whether an African worldview could exist among African Americans. It is noted that because many Africans have been living in America for several centuries, most African traditions are lost due to the socialization process (Belgrave & Allison, 2014). However, scholars posit that it is expected that Africentric worldview dimensions will be found to some degree among most people of African descent (e.g., Belgrave & Allison, 2014; Dudley-Grant, 2016). For this reason, understanding the broad aspects of Afrocentrism is helpful. Morris (2001) states that when clinicians and diagnosticians are in a better "listening" mode with respect to their clients, they can interpret information from within the context of their clients' cultural experiences. This skill is highly important to enhance the therapeutic relationship and treatment success when working with African American clients. Although the focus of this chapter is discussing Afrocentric dimensions, it is noted that many of the cultural beliefs and characteristics are found among other ethnic groups. Belgrave and Allison (2014) indicate that Latinos, Native Americans, and Asians may hold similar cultural beliefs that are consistent with Afrocentrism and collective cultures.

COLLECTIVISM

One of the central concepts that may influence interactions within the African American community is collectivism. Given the historical significance of community and maintaining group survival, it is possible that approaching clients from a Eurocentic or individualistic worldview may clash with the clients' belief system. According to Morris (2001), using a Eurocentric worldview can create one set of assumptions about the client and their sociocultural experiences that will differ from the set of assumptions made if the worldview is Afrocentric. Therefore, it is incumbent on the mental health provider to understand and explore how a collective orientation is important in the client's life. From an Afrocentric perspective, collectivism involves interdependence, cooperation, and working for the survival of the group rather than for the survival of the individual (Belgrave & Allison, 2014). In collectivist cultures, the individual and the individual's community both influence each other. Interpersonal interactions are important because an individual's own well-being is interconnected with that of the group (Belgrave & Allison, 2014). A common view within the African American community is that when one member suffers, everyone suffers, and when one member is doing well, everyone is doing well. This may serve as a potential strength but may also be additional sources of stress to consider when working with African American clients.

Among many African Americans, collective orientation is reflected through strong commitment to the family, the extended family, and fictive kin (e.g., Belgrave & Allison, 2014; Boyd-Franklin, 2003). Fictive kin are described as individuals who are not blood related or family through marriage but are treated as family (e.g., Boyd-Franklin, 2003). Fictive kin relationships may be an important source of social support and may be involved in caretaking. Due to the importance of family and community, individualistic values are not always appropriate when working with African Americans because much of Western psychology has focused on addressing problems at the individual level (Belgrave & Allison, 2014). However, more research on African Americans is needed to understand the existence of collectivism and individualism within this group.

Extended family is an important cultural consideration. The process of helping each other or reciprocity often involves sharing support as well as goods and services (Boyd-Franklin, 2003). Reciprocity may come in the form of lending money, taking care of a relative's child, or providing emotional support. It is important to evaluate healthy reciprocity, since an imbalance can result in causing stress to the individual who is burdened (Boyd-Franklin, 2003). In the therapy environment, the mental health professional should take care to explore the dynamics of the family system (and extended family) and evaluate if the client feels supported in his or her relationships. While the African American family is considered to be a major source of strength, it is important for providers to understand cultural norms for a well-functioning family (Boyd-Franklin, 2003).

SPIRITUALITY AND RELIGION

Spirituality is a fundamental Afrocentric dimension and is interwoven in the lives of African people (Belgrave & Allison, 2014). For many people of African descent, spirituality is woven into their daily activities and is not separate from other aspects of one's life (Belgrave & Allison, 2014; Boyd-Franklin & Lockwood, 1999). Boyd-Franklin (2003) notes that many African Americans grow up in environments where they have learned to internalize a sense of spirituality, but not all individuals participate in organized religious activities (e.g., attending church). Religious practices among African Americans are reflected in the amount of time that they spend in church compared to other groups, and they are more likely to use spirituality to provide comfort and more likely to use religion for coping with stressful life situations (Belgrave & Allison, 2014). According to data, 87 percent of African Americans reported belonging to one or more religious groups (Belgrave & Allison, 2014). Mental health providers must be sensitive to understanding the role of religion and spirituality in the lives of many African Americans (Boyd-Franklin, 2003).

Anecdotally, in some of my own research, I have found that African Americans tend to report being more spiritual and more likely to engage in religious practices (e.g., prayer) compared to other ethnic groups (Turner & Gamez, 2018). This is consistent with decades of research that has found that for African Americans, religion and church involvement are central components to their belief system (e.g., Boyd-

Franklin, 2003). Careful understanding and assessment of the role of spirituality in the lives of African American clients is imperative for healing. Some scholars articulate how spirituality serves an integral function in the survival of many African Americans (Boyd-Franklin, 2003), and this may consequently play out in the therapy process. For African Americans who have a strong sense of spiritual beliefs, it may serve as a barrier to treatment engagement and may lead to premature termination if the provider does not empower the client to also use this strength as a coping source along with therapy.

In the past, I have worked with clients who come to treatment expressing a strong spiritual belief system. Looking back on some of these early experiences, I can see how my training as a therapist from a Western perspective may have caused some difficulties with establishing rapport. I recall on a few occasions when a client inquired about my own personal religious affiliation or spiritual beliefs. Given my training on not disclosing personal information, I typically handled those situations with care and avoided directly answering the client's questions regarding whether I was "a spiritual or religious person." In hindsight, it is clear that the clients were attempting to understand my sense of openness to their belief systems and potentially exploring their own abilities to develop therapeutic relationships with me as their provider. According to Boyd-Franklin (2003), failure to recognize the importance of spiritual beliefs for some clients could result in impairing the joining process and impede therapy due to client resistance or lack of trust.

Spiritual reframing is a very useful technique with African American families (Boyd-Franklin, 2003; Boyd-Franklin & Lockwood, 1999). People who grow up in a "traditional Black community" may grow up with a system of core spiritual beliefs (Boyd-Franklin, 2003). Because of these core spiritual beliefs, African Americans may use spiritual reframing such as "God will work it out." This may increase reluctance to use therapy. Some posit that these spiritual beliefs highlight the strength of the person and can be used clinically to effectively address the client's difficulties (Boyd-Franklin, 2003). According to Boyd-Franklin (2003), a "therapist should feel free to inquire about the use of prayer and should even ask the client for examples of how she or he prays." This may help you understand the positive and negative attributes articulated in the client's prayer.

PERSPECTIVES ON TIME

Within the African American community, the concept of time is often attributed to the arrival of all of those attending an event. Time is viewed differently in Western cultures as opposed to African cultures (Belgrave & Allison, 2014). Scholars note that African cultures view time as being flexible and dictated by people rather than to being based on externally imposed events (Boyd-Franklin, 2003). Belgrave and Allison (2014) state that "European cultures view time as a commodity to be bought and sold; whereas among African cultures time is flexible and elastic, existing to meet the needs of the people." Taking a Eurocentric perspective is associated with a sense of urgency and pressure. According to Akbar (1991), this Eurocentric future-oriented perspective is inconsistent with African values. The concept of "colored people's time" (or CPT) is one of those values that exist within many collectivist cultures and is not specific to African Americans. CPT means that arriving late is acceptable or that things start when people arrive and end when people leave (Belgrave & Allison, 2014). This concept has been examined with empirical research and studies have demonstrated that many African Americans view time as "flexible" and not exact. Given the cultural significance of time, many African Americans have traditionally viewed time as more flexible. In a clinical setting, it is important to discuss expectations around treatment and session attendance. This might involve problem solving with African American clients to determine the best fit and to compromise to make therapy effective while being culturally sensitive.

EXPRESSIVE COMMUNICATION AND ORALITY

According to Belgrave and Allison (2014), the oral orientation often prescribed by African Americans historically helped slaves to retain the African culture in order to function in their new society. Historically, laws prevented African Americans from being able to read or write. Oral communication was often used in Africa to share information across generations from older to younger members (Belgrave & Allison, 2014). More research on preferences for oral versus nonformal methods for communicating in obtaining information among African

Americans is needed. Another important consideration is expression of affect and emotional connectedness. The sensitivity to affect and emotional cues is an orientation that acknowledges the emotional and affective state of self and others (Belgrave & Allison, 2014). This orientation places emphasis on emotional receptivity and expression. From this perspective, we have the ability to feel the pain and the joy of others and to expect others to feel our own pain and joy. For example, if a person feels happy, he or she is more likely to engage in positive behavior.

Verve and Rhythm

Verve and rhythm captures behavioral aspects of Africentricism. The concepts involve rhythmic behaviors and creativity through movement, posture, speech, and other behaviors (Belgrave & Allison, 2014; Boyd-Franklin, 2003). According to Belgrave and Allison (2014), "a person with verve walks, talks, and presents themselves in a creative and expressive way." Given the significance of these concepts, it is important to understand how it shapes learning styles and approaches to intervening in therapy. Verve suggests a preference for the simultaneous or novel experience of several stimuli rather than a singular and routine stimulus (Belgrave & Allison, 2014). Boykins and others (Belgrave & Allison, 2014; Boykins, 1983) note that when learning is consistent with verve and Afrocentric perspective, it involves multiple teaching methods and interactive learning (e.g., touching or expressiveness).

Harmony

According to African philosophy, balance and harmony are important aspects of one's overall mental, physical, and spiritual health (Belgrave & Allison, 2014). It is believed that all parts of an individual's life are interconnected. When there is imbalance between these components, it is assumed that one is not able to fully function. In African cultures, living in harmony also includes natural elements such as animals and plants (Belgrave & Allison, 2014). Black scholars note that the purpose of life is to live in harmony with animals and plants, as opposed to conquering them (Belgrave & Allison, 2014).

WORKING WITH AFRICAN DIASPORA SUBGROUPS

One of the challenges with working with African Americans is that they are often viewed as a monolithic group. In America, African Americans are often viewed the same regardless of their nationality or where they were born. However, this could create difficulties in therapy if the individual identifies more with their ancestry than race. Some individuals do not feel that the term "African American" captures their identity. These individuals may prefer to identify with their ethnic or cultural group due to their sense of loyalty and pride in their heritage (Black & Jackson, 2005). "African Americans" living in the United States could include people of African origins from Africa, South and Central America, the Caribbean, and elsewhere (Black & Jackson, 2005). The following section briefly describes some important considerations when working with individuals from the African diaspora that were born outside of the United States.

African Americans are 13 percent of the U.S. population and about 8 percent consist of Black immigrants from countries such as the Caribbean and Africa (Hall, 2017). There is limited research on clinical work with individuals from the West Indies or Jamaica, which may be due to outgroup invisibility. Therapy approaches for treatment among Caribbean populations is often from multiple theoretical orientations with limited research on the efficacy with this group (Dudley-Grant, 2016). According to Brice-Baker (2005), non-English-speaking Black people from the Caribbean or other countries may appear more culturally different, which requires more investigation. Much of the research on Caribbean psychology focuses on three subcultures: English-speaking Caribbeans, Spanish-speaking Caribbeans, and French-speaking Caribbeans (Dudley-Grant, 2016). According to Dudley-Grant (2016), practice with people of Caribbean descent requires that the provider be cognizant of "the use of psychotherapy in the services of several methods of population control, including assimilation, acculturation, and enculturation."

To be effective, mental health providers must be aware of the historical issues that influence the beliefs of people from the Caribbean and be respectful of values when implementing interventions (Dudley-Grant, 2016). Jamaicans often maintain the identity of their home country and identify themselves by the island where they were born (Brice-

Baker, 2005). Many people of Jamaican descent have different experiences than American Blacks since they lived in a predominately Black society before coming to the United States (Brice-Baker, 2005). Some scholars (Dudley-Grant, 2016) note that some people from the Caribbean may identify as White, which contributes to identity confusion and lack of self-definition. This identity confusion is stated to be the result of historical oppression. As a result, mental health providers should explore the individual's identity and work to understand how acculturation to the dominant society shapes his or her belief system.

In terms of mental health, cultural beliefs could lead to potential pitfalls. First, Jamaicans often do not recognize mental, psychological, or psychiatric problems (Brice-Baker, 2005; Dudley-Grant, 2016). What may be attributed to a mental health issue by mental health professionals may be perceived as a medical condition or spiritual disturbance in Jamaican families (Brice-Baker, 2005). Therapists are encouraged to become aware of the individual's cultural beliefs and to respect the decisions to seek help from healers, shamans, and other spiritual leaders (Dudley-Grant, 2016). This is particularly important when the mental health provider may not be from a Caribbean background or may have negative attitudes toward the clients' cultural practices. For example, Dudley-Grant (2016) states that mental health providers may not be open to the idea of voodoo or view it as "evil" instead of "healing."

Second, there may be a strong belief in using "withcraft" as a healing approach. One nontraditional method to treat mental health problems is through witchcraft or an obeah (i.e., witch doctor). An obeah is consulted to cure illness, predict the future, interpret dreams, allay fears, or grant favors (Brice-Baker, 2005). Brice-Baker (2005) notes that using an obeah is widespread throughout the island and by Jamaicans; they can be used to explain an unfavorable situation over which a client may feel that he or she has no control. Mental illness may be seen as a form of possession by evil spirits and individuals may seek help from a spiritual healer (Brice-Baker, 2005). The belief that mental illness results from an external demonic source is a common stigmatized belief (Dudley-Grant, 2016). People may also fear discrimination and stigma carrying over to family members as a result of being diagnosed with a mental disorder (Dudley-Grant, 2016).

One important concept to explore with individuals of Jamaican descent is family dynamics. Within the Caribbean family structure, views vary on parenting. Although there are similarities with African Americans that are born in the United States, subtle differences should be explored. Some communities believe children should be the central focus while others believe that they should be seen and not heard (Dudley-Grant, 2016). This concept may also be strongly held within the African American family. Family connections remain an important focus within the Caribbean family. A strong family connection with biological relatives and non-kin family members is associated with resilience across subcultures (Dudley-Grant, 2016). Nicolas, DeSilva, and Donnelly (2011) found that among a Haitian population, individuals who reported worries about a family member were at an increased risk for depressive symptoms.

Although evidence-based treatment options are limited, some modalities have been reported to be effective in addressing family issues (Dudley-Grant, 2016): multisystems family therapy, CAPAS (Criando con Amor: Promoviendo Armonía y Superación), and parent management training. Family therapy should include all individuals who provide critical influence on the child's life, those present or living apart (Dudley-Grant, 2016). Another consideration when treating people from the Caribbean is a preference for herbal remedies as opposed to prescription medications. According to Dudley-Grant (2016), natural remedies are more acceptable than expensive pharmaceuticals that may have unpleasant side effects. Family therapy may be the most effective treatment option because it is more consistent with cultural values (Dudley-Grant, 2016).

Jamaica is a society of gender role paradoxes. Sex roles are very traditional, varying little by class, race, or age (Brice-Baker, 2005). Girls are taught obedience, discouraged from being too assertive, and expected to be "pretty" but not "sexually alluring" (Brice-Baker, 2005). Boys are socialized to be responsible and obtain an education as a means to providing (Brice-Baker, 2005). Children are expected to have respect for their elders, and it is considered impolite to talk back or disagree with an older person (Brice-Baker, 2005). For more details about Caribbean Psychology refer to Dudley-Grant (2016).

ACCULTURATION AND ETHNIC IDENTITY

When working with clients of African descent, it is necessary to explore the individual's level of ethnic identity and acculturation. Numerous published articles have described how these variables influence mental health functioning and help-seeking (e.g., Obasi & Leong, 2009; Quintana, 2007; Turner et al., 2016). Typically, the literature has provided limited investigations of acculturation among African Americans. Obasi and Leong (2010) describe the significance of examining acculturation with people of African descent and articulate common acculturation strategies. Obasi and Leong (2010) provide the complete description of the Measurement of Acculturation Strategies for People of African Descent (MASPAD) that include strategies consistent with the acculturation literature (i.e., traditionalist, integrationist, assimilationist, and marginalist). The measure could be used in a clinical setting to help understand acculturation strategies. However, one caveat should be noted: limited research has been conducted to examine the concepts in non-U.S.-born people of African descent.

Finally, mental health providers should access the clients' level of ethnic identity. Cokley (2007) provides an overview of ethnic and racial identity. Although some scholars have occasionally used these concepts interchangeably, it is important to clarify the differences between the two constructs. Racial identity models tend to focus on physical features such as skin color, whereas ethnic identify focus on cultural factors or heritage. Clients may phenotypically be described as African American or Black, but there is a continuum to consider regarding connection and identification with one's ethnic group. Therapists—particularly those of non-African descent—must explore ethnic identity during the early stages of treatment. As discussed in the chapter on cultural competency, ethnic identity may impact the client-therapist relationship, psychological functioning, and adherence to Africentric worldview.

CONCLUSION

When working with clients of African descent, those born in the U.S. and those who have immigrated, it is important to understand within-group differences. As discussed, there are similarities among African Americans with respect to values and beliefs but people may adhere to those beliefs to different degrees. As a mental health practitioner, you should have an awareness of these different cultural values to improve your cultural responsiveness. However, you should avoid over-generalizing this information. Your knowledge about the different values and beliefs is helpful to assist you with exploring what values are most important to your client. Through collaboration between you and your client, you should grasp a better understand about the clients' cultural values and how it will influence treatment outcomes.

6

DEFINING THE FUTURE OF RESEARCH AND CLINICAL PRACTICE

Decades of research on the mental health profession have provided a substantial amount of information on working with ethnic minority populations. Early in my career, this information was instrumental in shaping my views on mental health, as well as providing me with a framework for offering mental health services. Since that time, the field has continued to advance to meet the needs of an increasingly diverse society. However, there remains room for growth to better train providers who work with people of African descent. Although we have made progress and moved away from our understanding of broad ethnic diversity to recognize the importance of within-group differences, there remains a gap when it comes to understanding some of the nuances when working with African American clients. The goal of this chapter is to discuss our current perspective and highlight implications for future directions in both conducting research and providing mental health services with this population.

Ethical responsibility must lead the way as we continue to advance as a mental health field. With that in mind, scholars and clinicians must work to avoid the most common ethical violations, such as lack of competence, lapses in maintaining self-awareness, and insensitivity when working with African American clients. Koocher and Keith-Spiegel (2008) note that insensitivity may involve lack of empathy, self-absorption, and prejudicial attitudes toward certain people. One might speculate that given the overrepresentation of non-White mental health professionals, especially at the doctoral level, these personal characteristics are extremely important to address. Ultimately changing these variables could prevent future damage and errors in our work as represented by historical ethical harm with this population. As noted earlier, mental health professionals should frequently consult their respective professional organizations' ethical codes (e.g., National Association for Social Workers, American Counseling Association, and American Association for Marriage and Family Therapy) for appropriate guidance.

As discussed earlier, race relations within the United States has often been difficult and many times these challenging interactions within society impact the therapeutic relationship with African American clients. This may be particularly true for White mental health professionals who are providing treatment to African Americans. Providers of color are not excluded from challenging situations due to the sociopolitical climate. In my own experience as an African American mental health professional, when there is tension due to race relations I have to make an extra effort to engage in my own self-care to ensure that I can be emotionally present for my clients. When African American clients are working with same-race mental health professionals, it may lead to some dynamics where the client may push boundary limits. Some research has shown that African American clinicians may struggle with these issues due to lack of training, living in communities where they offer services, or because they share some social networks (Goode-Cross, 2011; Goode-Cross & Grim, 2016).

As a field, mental health professionals generally recognize that many factors contribute to disparities in treatment-seeking, with African Americans being more likely to prematurely terminate or discontinue services. In my own research, I have found that many African Americans don't necessarily have negative perceptions about using services, but they tend to prefer seeking treatment that integrates their spiritual beliefs (Turner & Gamez, 2018). However, it is important that we understand each individual client's experience and avoid overgeneralizing this perspective to all African American clients. Although some clients may have a strong spiritual background and desire to have this discussed in treatment, others may not want this to be brought up during therapy. This is an area that should be further explored by research to understand what situations dictate when it is appropriate or not. For example, emerging research indicates that some African Americans do not want their therapist to bring up topics around religion (Turner & Cherry, 2019).

ADVANCES TO IMPROVE THE THERAPEUTIC ALLIANCE

One promising area of research and clinical practice that may be beneficial with African Americans is collaborative/therapeutic assessment (C/TA). For over 30 years, American psychologists have been discussing ways of using psychological assessment to promote therapeutic change by engaging clients in discussing their responses to psychological tests (Finn, Fischer, & Handler, 2012). Constance Fischer emphasized that collaborating with clients is a major means of individualizing the assessment process and identified the following principles (Finn, Fischer, & Handler, 2012):

- Collaborate: The assessor and client actively work together. The client is engaged as an active agent in discussing the purposes of the assessment, the meanings of her or his own test responses, useful next steps, and the written feedback that results at the end of the assessment.
- Contextualize: The clients' problems are explored in the context of their lived worlds, "from which they extend, grow, and change."
- Intervene: The goal is "not just to describe or classify the person's present state but to identify personally viable options to problematic behaviors." The primary goal of assessment should be to aid the client in identifying new ways of thinking and behaving.
- Describe: When writing reports, it is necessary to use the clients' own words to explain their behavior and functioning. This helps assessors and the readers find their way "into clients' worlds."
- Respect complexity, holism, and ambiguity: The goal of assessment is understanding rather than explanation. Therefore, the assessor should avoid reducing the client's life to variables or traits. It is important to respect the interconnectedness of all aspects of the client's life.

The main goal of C/TA is to use questions that the client asks as the starting point to get a glimpse into the "truth" of a client's life (Engelman et al., 2016). Engelman and colleagues (2016) state that the use of C/TA as a tool helps to act as "empathy magnifiers" and provides information about the client's strengths, struggles, and strivings at that moment in his or her life. Many clinicians often interpret assessments with African Americans at face value and clinically interpret the data without considering the environmental context. One of the reasons that applying therapeutic assessment is useful is because it helps to personalize the treatment process and break down African Americans' opinions about therapy being a one-size-fits-all approach to treatment and not being individualized. Finn (2007) suggested that "collaborative assessment be used when assessors strive to reduce the power imbalance typically found between assessor and client in traditional assessment."

According to Finn (2007) and others (e.g., DeSaeger et al., 2014; Tharinger, Finn, & Gentry, 2013), C/TA is a method that uses psychological assessment techniques to collaborate with the client by formulating assessment and treatment goals by using the client's questions about themselves as the centerpiece for conducting an assessment evaluation. As a clinical tool, C/TA uses assessment to capture the truth of the client's life by applying clinical training and experience in your work to reach a more accurate diagnosis and conceptualization. Finn and colleagues (Finn, 2007; Tharinger et al., 2009; Tharinger, Finn, & Gentry, 2013) have outlined a six-step general model of therapeutic assessment (TA) that can be applied to applied to children, adolescents, and adults that includes the following phases: (a) construction of assessment questions, (b) standardized psychological testing, (c) assessment intervention, (d) summary and discussion of findings, (e) written communication, and (f) followup. In C/TA, providers acknowledge the vulnerability of their clients in the assessment situation and try to minimize any unnecessary discomfort for clients (Finn, Fischer, & Handler, 2012).

Research has provided strong evidence for the role of the therapeutic relationship in conducting psychological evaluations and implementing treatments. C/TA has been shown to have positive effects with outpatient and inpatient clients facing a variety of difficulties and with adults, children, adolescents, and couples (Finn, Fischer, & Handler, 2012). Given these positive outcomes, C/TA may be one way to reduce biases in assessment and improve the likelihood of engaging African

Americans in treatment (Turner & Mills, 2016). To date, studies have found that the use of C/TA increases rapport with clients and has positive treatment outcomes when used as a short-term intervention (e.g., Austin, Krumholz, & Tharinger, 2012; De Saeger et al., 2014; Tharinger et al., 2009). De Saeger and colleagues (2014) most recently noted two randomized controlled studies demonstrating promising effects of C/TA interventions in reducing symptomatic distress and increasing self-esteem in college students. Furthermore, the authors noted the benefits of using a pretreatment TA intervention to improve outcomes. For example, clients who received the TA pretreatment intervention reported greater reductions in affective instability and suicidal ideation, as well as a marginally stronger working alliance than the treatment-as-usual group. Finn, Fischer, and Handler (2012) note that C/TA is generally associated with decreased symptomatology, increased self-esteem, better compliance with treatment recommendations, improved therapeutic alliance, and increased family cohesion and communication across multiple studies.

Although limited research exists on applying TA with African American clients, some research has demonstrated its utility with African American youth. Turner and Mills (2016) discuss that when TA is applied to youth, the goals of the approach include: (a) helping parents understand their child's psychological assessment findings and become more empathetic to their child's challenges and (b) guiding parents in changing their attitudes toward their child and improving their interactions to foster positive child and family development. To demonstrate the utility of TA, Guerrero, Lipkind, and Rosenberg (2011) conducted a case study with an 11-year-old African American girl to explore integrating issues around race and class in assessment and treatment. Overall, the authors concluded that the process was able to gather sufficient information to accurately diagnose the client and assist the family with identifying appropriate treatment options including community resources. For many African American clients, it is pivotal that the mental health provider takes on roles, such as helping them navigate community resources (e.g., school referrals).

When using C/TA, there are several additional considerations that are important. Research on providing feedback suggest applying multiple levels when discussing assessment results (Finn, 2007; Guerrero, Lipkind, & Rosenberg, 2011). Finn (2007) identifies three levels of feedback: Level 1 findings—those that the client can easily accept and verify themselves; Level 2 findings—those that tend to modify the client's way of thinking or amplify the ways that they think about themselves; and Level 3 findings—information difficult for the client to tolerate and that he or she might reject or deny. Generally, it appears that using C/TA with African Americans has the potential to improve psychological assessment and diagnosis with this population.

CURRENT KNOWLEDGE OF CULTURALLY ADAPTED TREATMENTS

As discussed in chapter 4, cultural adaptations of evidence-based treatments should be considered when working with African Americans. According to Domenech Rodríguez and Bernal (2012), cultural adaptations are useful because they make an explicit understanding of other cultures and prescribe how being influenced by others can enhance our knowledge of others as an avenue to create a sense of "we." Research on multicultural competence or cultural sensitivity has been instrumental in increasing providers' attention to the importance of cultural competence in conducting research and providing mental health treatment with ethnic and racial populations, but there remains a need for more evidence-based interventions with diverse minority populations (Hays, 2009).

Scholars have stressed the importance of culturally sensitive interventions to increase engagement among African Americans in therapy to improve outcomes (Hall et al., 2016; Jones, Huey, & Rubenson, 2018). However, limited research currently exists on cultural adaptions with this population. Jones, Huey, and Rubenson (2018) identify some support for the efficacy of evidence-based treatments with African Americans. Despite the limitations that have been discussed, treatment with African Americans is primarily standardized treatment approaches or a version that is modified to be more culturally sensitive. Domenech Rodríguez and Bernal (2012) describe summaries of existing models, frameworks, and guidelines for cultural adaptation of psychological interventions. The authors highlight 12 models or frameworks of cultural adaptations that were published between 2004 and 2016. In general, scholars who developed these frameworks built upon existing research to incorporate cultural variables such as acculturation, discrimination, immigration, spirituality, and cultural values (Domenech Rodríguez & Bernal, 2012). Although a full description of these models and frameworks are outside of the scope of this book, you can refer to Bernal and Domenech Rodríguez (2012) for a complete discussion.

According to Domenech Rodríguez and Bernal (2012), in the mid-1990s, scholars began to develop recommendations for cultural adaptations and the majority were developed in isolation. However, it appears that each of the models or frameworks attempts to consider the role of the mental health provider and how the intervention characteristics can improve ecological validity. The following brief description identifies some of the common cultural adaptation models.

- The Multidimensional Model of Understanding Culturally Responsive Psychotherapies (Koss-Chioino & Vargas, 1992) describes how all therapy approaches can be developed to consider two dimensions: culture (cultural content and cultural context) and structure (steps or changes that produce a particular result in psychotherapy and the manner or style of carrying out psychotherapy).
- The Ecological Validity Framework (EVF) (Bernal, Bonilla, & Bellido, 1995) is based on the ecological systems theory and recommends eight areas for consideration in culturally adapting and intervention: language, persons, metaphors, content, concepts, goals, methods, and context.
- The Cultural Accommodation Model (CAM) (Leong & Lee, 2006) describes a three-step process to cultural adaptation: identifying cultural gaps, gathering relevant literature to fill the gaps, and testing the new theory or intervention to check for improved validity.
- The Cultural Sensitivity Framework (CSF) (Resnicow, Soler, Braithwaite, Ahwluwalia, & Butler, 2002) seeks to integrate ethnic/cultural characteristics, experiences, norms, values, behavioral patterns, and beliefs of a target population as well as relevant historical, environmental, and social forces into the design, delivery, and evaluation of the health promotion materials and programs. One of the benefits of the CSF is that it emphasizes both surface (visual modifications to the materials and intervention content for the target group) and deep adaptations (addressing

sociohistorical, psychological, environmental, and cultural components).

When examining the literature on culturally adapted interventions, the majority of the studies use a top-down approach to modify standard intervention approaches to treat African American clients. An evidence-based intervention is considered "top down" when an intervention is developed for one group and modified for application to another group (Hall et al., 2016). Although research supports this type of adaptation, some scholars express concerns about modifying standard intervention for treatment of diverse groups. According to Hall and colleagues (2016), "if generic interventions are sufficiently effective among diverse groups, then adapting interventions to boost cultural fit for specific groups comes at an unnecessary cost. Adapted interventions risk losing their connection to the evidence base that was originally established for the intervention."

When evaluating the research on culturally adapted intervention, effect sizes from meta-analyses have been found to be heterogeneous and moderated by variables such as client age, client/therapist ethnic match, language of intervention (i.e., English vs. non-English), client acculturation, psychopathology outcome, and study design (Hall et al., 2016). To further explore the efficacy and effectiveness of culturally adapted interventions, Hall and colleagues (2016) conducted a meta-analysis using 78 studies conducted in the last 20 years. Of the studies included, 29 percent of the participants were African American or African. The authors concluded that culturally adapted intervention produced greater reductions in symptoms than other interventions or no intervention control groups (as supported by a medium effect size). The majority of the studies in the meta-analysis were also identified as using a top-down approach (only four used a bottom-up approach). Table 6.1 identifies culturally adapted interventions with African Americans. It should be noted that there is a huge gap in terms of the research on African, Afro-Caribbean, and Haitian populations. Only two of the studies cited used an international population and limited studies include subpopulations such as individuals from Haiti. As discussed earlier in chapter 4, more research is needed to improve our understanding of evidence-based and culturally adapted interventions with African Americans.

Table 6.1. Culturally Adapted Interventions with African Americans

Reference	Sample	Treatment	Results
Afuwape et al. (2010)[*]	Black adults	CBT	At 3-month follow-up, decreased depression.
Banks et al. (1996)	African American youth	Social skills training	SST and Afrocentric SST groups showed decreased anger and increased assertiveness/self-control.
Bella-Awusah et al. (2015)[*]	African youth in Southwest Nigeria	School-based CBT	At 1-week and 16-week follow-ups, decreased depression symptoms.
Brody et al. (2006)	African American youth	Strong African American Families Program	At post-intervention, improved parent communication and decreased youth risky behavior.
Carter et al. (2003)	African American women	CBT group therapy	At post-intervention, decreased panic attacks, decreased anxiety, and decreased avoidance behavior.
Feske (2008)	African American and European American women	Prolonged exposure	At post-intervention, decreased posttraumatic stress disorder, anxiety, and depression symptoms.
Ginsburg & Drake (2002)	African American youth	CBT group therapy	At post-treatment, decreased social anxiety.
Grote et al. (2009)	African American and European American women	Brief interpersonal therapy	At post-intervention and 6-month follow-up, decreased depression for both groups.
Henggeler, Melton, & Smith (1992)	African American, Latino, and European American youth	MST	At follow-up, increased family cohesion and decreased aggression.
Henggeler, Pickrel, & Brondino (1999)	African American, Latino, Asian American, and European American youth	MST	At post-intervention and 6-month follow-up, reduced substance use and reductions in criminal activity.
Huey et al. (2004)	African American and European American youth	MST	At post-intervention and 1-year follow-up, decreased suicide attempts.

Jones (2008)	African American women	Claiming Your Connection group intervention	At post-intervention, decreased depression.
Jones & Warner (2011)	African American women	Claiming Your Connection group intervention	At post-intervention, decreased depression and stress.
Kaslow et al. (2010)	African American women	Nia psycho-educational group intervention	At post-intervention, 6- and 12-month follow-ups, decreased depression.
Liddle et al. (2004)	African American, Latino, Haitian American, Jamaican American, and European American youth	Multi-dimensional family therapy	At post-intervention, increased family cohesion and decreased substance use.

˚international study

CBT = cognitive behavioral therapy

MST = multisystemic therapy

Source: Hall et al., 2016.

CONCLUSION

Overall, the field has clearly identified barriers to help-seeking and approaches to increase treatment engagement with African Americans. In applying the Model of Treatment Initiation (MTI) (Turner et al., 2016; Turner, Malone, & Douglas, 2019), we must consider the interaction of how these variables differently impact treatment among African Americans. Based on the MTI conceptualization, major influences may include accessibility factors (structural variables that may influence an individual's ability to access treatment), availability factors (access to culturally competent services), appropriateness factors (how individuals view mental health problems as requiring treatment), and acceptability factors (variables such as stigma and cultural mistrust). Some of these factors might contribute to help-seeking while others may inhibit treatment engagement or retention. To address these concerns, it is necessary for mental health providers to explore their clients' attitudes and perceptions at the outset of treatment. Furthermore, skills in cultural competency as well as culturally adapted interventions should be an important consideration.

As discussed earlier in the chapter, both the intervention approach (standard versus culturally adapted) and the therapeutic alliance are pivotal to treatment success with African Americans. Although the field has made progress toward being more culturally sensitive, there is still room for improvement. Particularly in regard to training mental health professionals and increasing research to examine the efficacy and effectiveness of treatments with this population. Given the gaps with evidence-based practice, Hall and colleagues (2016) have offered some considerations for future directions.

1. It is crucial to identify and measure community-specific cultural contexts of risk and resilience that influence disorders because this component of cultural adaptation has been largely neglected. These risk and resilience contexts should guide efforts to design and evaluate culturally adapted interventions.
2. The effects of top-down cultural adaptations on both mainstream and culture-specific psychopathology outcomes need to be further evaluated in comparisons of culturally adapted versus standard forms of the same intervention. An adequate evaluation of cultural adaptations should focus on substantive modifications that are likely to produce differences (e.g., cultural content and values) rather than on relatively minor variations (e.g., therapist-client ethnic match, language translation).
3. The effects of bottom-up interventions versus evidence-based interventions on both mainstream and culture-specific psychopathology outcomes need to be evaluated. Bottom-up interventions may already exist in community settings but have not been evaluated. Rather than reinvent the wheel, researchers should increase partnerships with community mental health organizations to empirically evaluate community-specific, bottom-up approaches.
4. Careful examination of potential moderators of intervention effects associated with therapists (e.g., cultural competence) and clients (e.g., racial/ethnic identity) is needed. It is likely that therapist and client personal characteristics account for

moderation of intervention effects more than surface variables, such as therapist ethnicity or language in which the intervention is conducted.

5. Ethnic/race-related disparities in mental health service utilization have been well-documented and persistent. Research on how cultural adaptations affect participant engagement in interventions is necessary. (p. 17)

REFERENCES

Afuwape, S. A., Craig, T. K., Harris, T., Clarke, M., Flood, A., Olajide, D., Cole, E., Leese, M., McCrone, P., & Thornicroft, G. (2010). The Cares of Life Project (CoLP): An exploratory randomised controlled trial of a community-based intervention for black people with common mental disorder. *Journal of Affective Disorders, 127*, 370–74.

Ajzen, I. (1991). The theory of planned behavior. *Organizational Behavior and Human Decision Processes, 50*(2), 179–211.

Akbar, N. I. (1991). The evolution of human psychology for African Americans. In R. Jones (Ed.), *Black Psychology* (pp. 99–123). Berkeley, CA: Cobb & Henry.

Akbar, M., Chambers, J. W., Jr., & Thompson, V. L. S. (2001). Racial identity, Africentric values, and self-esteem in Jamaican children. *Journal of Black Psychology, 27*(3), 341–58.

American Psychological Association. (1990). *Guidelines for providers of psychological services to ethnic, linguistic, and culturally diverse populations.* Washington, DC: Author.

American Psychological Association. (2002). *Guidelines on multicultural education, training, research, practice, and organizational change for psychologists.* Washington, DC: Author.

American Psychological Association. (2003). Guidelines on multicultural education, training, research, practice, and organizational change for psychologists. *American Psychologist, 58*, 377–402.

American Psychological Association. (2017a). *Ethical Principles for Psychologists and Code of Conduct.* Retrieved from https://www.apa.org/ethics/code/.

American Psychological Association, APA Working Group on Stress and Health Disparities. (2017b). Stress and health disparities: Contexts, mechanisms, and interventions among racial/ethnic minority and low-socioeconomic status populations. Retrieved from http://www.apa.org/pi/health-disparities/resources/stress-report.aspx.

American Psychological Association. (2017c). *Multicultural Guidelines: An Ecological Approach to Context, Identity, and Intersectionality.* Retrieved from http://www.apa.org/about/policy/multicultural-guidelines.pdf.

American Psychological Association. (2017d). Demographics of U.S. psychology workforce. Retrieved from http://www.apa.org/workforce/data-tools/demographics.aspx.

American Psychological Association. (2018, August 22). APA Launches Video on Race-Related Stress. Retrieved from https://www.apa.org/news/press/releases/2018/08/race-related-stress.

Andersen, R. M. (1995). Revisiting the behavioral model and access to medical care: Does it matter? *Journal of Health and Social Behavior*, 1–10.

Anderson, R., Jones, S., Navarro, C., McKenny, M., Mehta, T., & Stevenson, H. (2018). Addressing the mental health needs of Black American youth and families: A case study from the EMBRace intervention. *International Journal of Environmental Research and Public Health, 15*(5), 898.

Anderson, R. E., McKenny, M., Mitchell, A., Koku, L., & Stevenson, H. C. (2018). EMBRacing racial stress and trauma: Preliminary feasibility and coping responses of a racial socialization intervention. *Journal of Black Psychology, 44*(1), 25–46.

Anderson, R. E., & Stevenson, H. C. (2019). RECASTing racial stress and trauma: Theorizing the healing potential of racial socialization in families. *American Psychologist, 74*(1), 63–75.

Arredondo, P. (1999). Multicultural counseling competencies as tools to address oppression and racism. *Journal of Counseling & Development, 77*(1), 102–8.

Arredondo, P., & Toporek, R. (2004). Multicultural counseling competencies = ethical practice. *Journal of Mental Health Counseling, 26*(1), 44–55.

Austin, C. A., Krumholz, L. S., & Tharinger, D. J. (2012). Therapeutic assessment with an adolescent: Choosing connections over substances. *Journal of Personality Assessment, 94*(6), 571–85.

Baldwin, J. A. (1986). African (Black) psychology: Issues and synthesis. *Journal of Black Studies, 16*(3), 235–49.

Banks, R., Hogue, A., Timberlake, T., & Liddle, H. (1996). An Afrocentric approach to group social skills training with inner-city African-American adolescents. *Journal of Negro Education, 65*, 414–23.

Belgrave, F. Z., & Allison, K. W. (2014). Psychosocial adaptation and mental health. *African American Psychology: From Africa to America* (pp. 409–44). Thousand Oaks, CA: Sage Publications.

Belgrave, F. Z., Brome, D. R., & Hampton, C. (2000). The contribution of Africentric values and racial identity to the prediction of drug knowledge, attitudes, and use among African American youth. *Journal of Black Psychology, 26*(4), 386–401.

Bella-Awusah, T., Ani, C., Ajuwon, A., & Omigbodun, O. (2015). Effectiveness of brief school-based, group cognitive behavioural therapy for depressed adolescents in southwest Nigeria. *Child and Adolescent Mental Health, 21*, 44–50.

Bernal, G., & Adames, C. (2017). Cultural adaptations: Conceptual, ethical, contextual and methodological issues for working with ethnocultural and majority-world populations. *Prevention Science, 18*, 681–88.

Bernal, G., & Domenech Rodríguez, M. M. (2012). *Cultural adaptations: Tools for evidence-based practice with diverse populations.* Washington, DC: American Psychological Association.

Bernard, D. L., Lige, Q. M., Willis, H. A., Sosoo, E. E., & Neblett, E. W. (2017). Impostor phenomenon and mental health: The influence of racial discrimination and gender. *Journal of Counseling Psychology, 64*(2), 155–66.

Black, L., & Jackson, V. (2005). Families of African origin. In M. McGoldrick, J. Giordano, & N. Garcia-Preto (Eds.), *Ethnicity and Family Therapy* (pp. 77–86). New York: Guilford Press.

Bor, J., Venkataramani, A. S., Williams, D. R., & Tsai, A. C. (2018). Police killings and their spillover effects on the mental health of Black Americans: A population-based, quasi-experimental study. *The Lancet, 392*, 302–10.

Boyd-Franklin, N. (2003). *Black families in therapy: Understanding the African American experience.* 2nd Ed. New York: Guilford Press.

Boyd-Franklin, N. (2010). Incorporating spirituality and religion into the treatment of African American clients. *The Counseling Psychologist, 38*(7), 976–1000.

Boyd-Franklin, N., & Lockwood, T. W. (1999). Spirituality and religion: Implications for psychotherapy with African American clients and families. In F. Walsh (Ed.), *Spiritual Resources in Family Therapy* (pp. 90–103). New York: Guilford Press.

Boykin, A. W., Jagers, R. J., Ellison, C. M., & Albury, A. (1997). Communalism: Conceptualization and measurement of an Afrocultural social orientation. *Journal of Black Studies, 27*(3), 409–18.

Boykin, W. (1983). The academic performance of Afro-American children. In J. Spence (Ed.), *Achievement and achievement motives.* San Francisco: Freeman.

Brice-Baker, J. R. (2005). British West Indian families. In M. McGoldrick, J. Giordano, & N. Garcia-Preto (Eds.), *Ethnicity and Family Therapy* (pp. 117–25). New York: Guilford Press.

Brody, G. H., Murry, V. M., Gerrard, M., Gibbons, F. X., McNair, L., Brown, A. C., Wills T. A., Molgaard V., Spoth R. L., Luo Z., & Chen, Y. F. (2006). The strong African American families program: Prevention of youths' high-risk behavior and a test of a model of change. *Journal of Family Psychology, 20*, 1–11.

Bryant-Davis, T., & Ocampo, C. (2005). Racist incident-based trauma. *The Counseling Psychologist, 33*(4), 479–500.

Bryant-Davis, T., Adams, T., Alejandre, A., & Gray, A. A. (2017). The trauma lens of police violence against racial and ethnic minorities. *Journal of Social Issues, 73*(4), 852–71.

Carlson, E. B. (2001). Psychometric study of a brief screen for PTSD: Assessing the impact of multiple traumatic events. *Assessment, 8*(4), 431–41.

Carter, M. M., Sbrocco, T., Gore, K. L., Watt Marin, N., & Lewis, E. L. (2003). Cognitive-behavioural group therapy versus a wait-list control in the treatment of African-American women with panic disorder. *Cognitive Therapy and Research, 27*, 505–18.

Carter, R. T. (2007). Racism and psychological and emotional injury: Recognizing and assessing race-based traumatic stress. *The Counseling Psychologist, 35*(1), 13–105.

Carter, R. T., Mazzula, S., Victoria, R., Vazquez, R., Hall, S., Smith, S., Sant-Barket, S., Forsyth, J., Bazelais, K., & Williams, B. (2013). Initial development of the race-based traumatic stress symptom scale: Assessing the emotional impact of racism. *Psychological Trauma: Theory, Research, Practice, and Policy, 5*(1), 1–9.

Chen, E. C., Kakkad, D., & Balzano, J. (2008). Multicultural competence and evidence-based practice in group therapy. *Journal of Clinical Psychology, 64*(11), 1261–78.

Chu, J., Leino, A., Pflum, S., & Sue, S. (2016). A model for the theoretical basis of cultural competency to guide psychotherapy. *Professional Psychology: Research and Practice, 47*(1), 18–29.

Cokley, K. (2007). Critical issues in the measurement of ethnic and racial identity: A referendum on the state of the field. *Journal of Counseling Psychology, 54*(3), 224–34.

Cokley, K., McClain, S., Enciso, A., & Martinez, M. (2013). An examination of the impact of minority status stress and impostor feelings on the mental health of diverse ethnic minority college students. *Journal of Multicultural Counseling and Development, 41*(2), 82–95.

Comas-Díaz, L., Hall, G. N., Neville, H. A., & Kazak, A. E. (2019). Racial trauma: Theory, research, and healing. *American Psychologist, 74*(1).

Constantine, M. G. (2007). Racial microaggressions against African American clients in cross-racial counseling relationships. *Journal of Counseling Psychology, 54*(1), 1–16.

Constantine, M. G., Lewis, E. L., Conner, L. C., & Sanchez, D. (2000). Addressing spiritual and religious issues in counseling African Americans: Implications for counselor training and practice. *Counseling and Values, 45*(1), 28–38.

Constantine, M. G., Smith, L., Redington, R. M., & Owens, D. (2008). Racial microaggressions against Black counseling and counseling psychology faculty: A central challenge in the multicultural counseling movement. *Journal of Counseling & Development, 86*(3), 348–55.

Constantine, M. G., & Sue, D. W. (2007). Perceptions of racial microaggressions among Black supervisees in cross-racial dyads. *Journal of Counseling Psychology, 54*(2), 142–53.

Corbie-Smith, G. (1999). The continuing legacy of the Tuskegee syphilis study: Considerations for clinical investigation. *American Journal of Medical Science, 317*(1), 5–8

Davis, S. P., Arnette, N. C., Bethea, K. S., Graves, K. N., Rhodes, M. N., Harp, S. E., Dunn, Sarah E., Patel, M. N., & Kaslow, N. J. (2009). The Grady Nia Project: A culturally competent intervention for low-income, abused, and suicidal African American women. *Professional Psychology: Research and Practice, 40*(2), 141–47.

De Saeger, H., Kamphuis, J. H., Finn, S. E., Smith, J. D., Verheul, R., van Busschbach, J. J., Feenstra, D. J., & Horn, E. K. (2014). Therapeutic assessment promotes treatment readiness but does not affect symptom change in patients with personality disorders: Findings from a randomized clinical trial. *Psychological Assessment, 26*(2), 474–83.

Dudley-Grant, R. (2016). Innovations in clinical psychology with Carribbean peoples. In J. L. Roopnarine and D. Chadee (Eds.), *Caribbean Psychology: Indigenous Contributions to a Global Discipline.* Washington, DC: American Psychological Association.

Engelman, D. H., Allyn, J. B., Crisi, A., Finn, S. E., Fischer, C. T., & Nakamura, N. (2016). "Why am I so stuck?": A collaborative/therapeutic assessment case discussion. *Journal of Personality Assessment, 98*(4), 360–73.

Epstein, A. M., & Ayanian, J. Z. (2001). Racial disparities in medical care. *New England Journal of Medicine, 344*(19), 1471–73.

Fairchild, A. L., & Bayer, R. (1999). Uses and abuses of Tuskegee. *Science, 284*(5416), 919–21.

Feske, U. (2008). Treating low-income and minority women with posttraumatic stress disorder: A pilot study comparing prolonged exposure and treatment as usual conducted by community therapists. *Journal of Interpersonal Violence, 23,* 1027–40.

Finn, S. E. (2007). *In Our Clients' Shoes: Theory and Techniques of Therapeutic Assessment.* Mahwah, NJ: Lawrence Erlbaum Associates.

Finn, S. E., Fischer, C. T., & Handler, L. (2012). *Collaborative/Therapeutic Assessment: A Casebook and Guide.* Hoboken, NJ: Wiley.

Franklin-Jackson, D., & Carter, R. T. (2007). The relationships between race-related stress, racial identity, and mental health for Black Americans. *Journal of Black Psychology, 33*(1), 5–26.

Freimuth, V. S., Quinn, S. C., Thomas, S. B., Cole, G., Zook, E., & Duncan, T. (2001). African Americans' views on research and the Tuskegee syphilis study. *Social Science and Medicine, 52,* 797–808.

Gallardo, M. E. (Ed.). (2013). *Developing Cultural Humility: Embracing Race, Privilege and Power.* Thousand Oaks, CA: Sage Publications.

Galovski, T. E., Peterson, Z. D., Beagley, M. C., Strasshofer, D. R., Held, P., & Fletcher, T. D. (2016). Exposure to violence during Ferguson protests: Mental health effects for law enforcement and community members. *Journal of Traumatic Stress, 29*(4), 283–92.

Gilligan, C. (1982). New maps of development: New visions of maturity. *American Journal of Orthopsychiatry, 52*(2), 199–212.

Ginsburg, G. S., & Drake, K. L. (2002). School-based treatment for anxious African-American adolescents: A controlled pilot study. *Journal of the American Academy of Child & Adolescent Psychiatry, 41,* 768–75

Goode-Cross, D. T. (2011). Same difference: Black therapists' experience of same-race therapeutic dyads. *Professional Psychology: Research and Practice, 42*(5), 368–74.

Goode-Cross, D. T., & Grim, K. A. (2016). "An unspoken level of comfort": Black therapists' experiences working with Black clients. *Journal of Black Psychology, 42*(1), 29–53.

Gooden, A. S., & McMahon, S. D. (2016). Thriving among African-American adolescents: Religiosity, religious support, and communalism. *American Journal of Community Psychology, 57*(1–2), 118–128.

Grier, W. H., & Cobbs, P. M. (1968). *Black rage.* New York: Basic Books.

Grills, C. (2004). African psychology. In R. Jones (Ed.), *African psychology* (pp. 171–208). Hampton, VA: Cobb and Henry.

Grote, N. K., Swartz, H. A., Geibel, S. L., Zuckoff, A., Houck, P. R., & Frank, E. (2009). A randomized controlled trial of culturally relevant, brief interpersonal psychotherapy for perinatal depression. *Psychiatric Services, 60,* 313–21

Guerrero, B., Lipkind, J., & Rosenberg, A. (2011). Why did she put nail polish in my drink?: Applying the therapeutic assessment model with an African American foster child in a community mental health setting. *Journal of Personality Assessment, 93*(1), 7–15.

Guthrie, R. (1976). *Even the Rat Was White.* New York: Harper & Row.

Haas, L. J., Malouf, J. L., & Mayerson, N. H. (1986). Ethical dilemmas in psychological practice: Results of a national survey. *Professional Psychology: Research and Practice, 17*(4), 316–21.

Hall, G. C. N. (2017). *Multicultural psychology* (3rd Edition). New York: Routledge.

Hall, G. C. N., Ibaraki, A. Y., Huang, E. R., Marti, C. N., & Stice, E. (2016). A meta-analysis of cultural adaptations of psychological interventions. *Behavior Therapy, 47*(6), 993–1014.

Hamilton, A. M., Fowler, J. L., Hersh, B., Austin, C. A., Finn, S. E., Tharinger, D. J., Parton, V., Stahl, K., & Arora, P. (2009). "Why won't my parents help me?": Therapeutic Assessment of a child and her family. *Journal of Personality Assessment*, *91*(2), 108–20.

Harrell, S. P. (2000). A multidimensional conceptualization of racism-related stress: Implications for the well-being of people of color. *American Journal of Orthopsychiatry*, *70*(1), 42–57.

Harris-Britt, A., Valrie, C. R., Kurtz-Costes, B., & Rowley, S. J. (2007). Perceived racial discrimination and self-esteem in African American youth: Racial socialization as a protective factor. *Journal of Research on Adolescence*, *17*(4), 669–82.

Hays, P. A. (2009). Integrating evidence-based practice, cognitive-behavior therapy, and multicultural therapy: Ten steps for culturally competent practice. *Professional Psychology: Research and Practice*, *40*(4), 354–60.

Helms, J. E., Nicolas, G., & Green, C. E. (2010). Racism and ethnoviolence as trauma: Enhancing professional training. *Traumatology*, *16*(4), 53–62.

Henggeler, S. W., Melton, G. B., & Smith, L. A. (1992). Family preservation using multisystemic therapy: An effective alternative to incarcerating serious juvenile offenders. *Journal of Consulting and Clinical Psychology*, *60*, 953–61.

Henggeler, S. W., Pickrel, S. G., & Brondino, M. J. (1999). Multisystemic treatment of substance abusing and dependent delinquents: Outcomes, treatment fidelity, and transportability. *Mental Health Services Research*, *1*, 171–84.

Hines-Martin, V., Malone, M., Kim, S., & Brown-Piper, A. (2003). Barriers to mental health care access in an African American population. *Issues in Mental Health Nursing*, *24*, 237–56.

Holden, K. B., & Xanthos, C. (2009). Disadvantages in mental health care among African Americans. *Journal of Health Care for the Poor and Underserved*, *20*(2), 17–23.

Holmes, M. D. (2000). Minority threat and police brutality: Determinants of civil rights criminal complaints in U.S. municipalities. *Criminology*, *38*(2), 343–68.

Horwitz, A. (1978). Family, kin, and friend networks in psychiatric help-seeking. *Social Science & Medicine. Part A: Medical Psychology & Medical Sociology*, *12*, 297–304.

Huey, S. J., Jr., Henggeler, S. W., Rowland, M. D., Halliday-Boykins, C., Cunningham, P. B., Pickrel, S. G., & Edwards, J. (2004). Multisystemic therapy effects on attempted suicide by youths presenting psychiatric emergencies. *Journal of the American Academy of Child and Adolescent Psychiatry*, *43*, 183–90.

Hurst, A. N., Bailey, M. L., Krueger, N. T., Garba, R., & Cokley, K. (2017). The psychological impact of policing on African American students. In *Law Enforcement in the Age of Black Lives Matter: Policing Black and Brown Bodies* (pp. 53–73). Lanham, MD: Lexington Books.

Jackson-Gilfort, A., Liddle, H. A., Tejeda, M. J., & Dakof, G. A. (2001). Facilitating engagement of African American male adolescents in family therapy: A cultural theme process study. *Journal of Black Psychology*, *27*(3), 321–40.

Jones, E., Huey, S. J., & Rubenson, M. (2018). Cultural competence in therapy with African Americans. In C. L. Frisby & W. T. O'Donohue (Eds.), *Cultural Competence in Applied Psychology* (pp. 557–73). New York: Springer International Publishing, Inc.

Jones, J. H. (1993). *Bad Blood: The Tuskegee Syphilis Experiment*. New York: The Free Press

Jones, L. V. (2008). Preventing depression: Culturally relevant group work with Black women. *Research on Social Work Practice*, *18*, 626–34.

Jones, L. V., & Warner, L. A. (2011). Evaluating culturally responsive group work with Black women. *Research on Social Work Practice*, *21*, 737–46.

Jones, S. C., & Neblett, E. W. (2017). Future directions in research on racism-related stress and racial-ethnic protective factors for Black youth. *Journal of Clinical Child & Adolescent Psychology*, *46*(5), 754–66.

Joseph, N., Watson, N. N., Wang, Z., Case, A. D., & Hunter, C. D. (2013). Rules of engagement: Predictors of Black Caribbean immigrants' engagement with African American culture. *Cultural Diversity and Ethnic Minority Psychology*, *19*(4), 414–23.

Kaslow, N. J., Leiner, A. S., Reviere, S., Jackson, E., Bethea, K., Bhaju, J., Rhodes, M., Gantt, M. J., Senter, H., & Thompson, M. P. (2010). Suicidal, abused African American women's response to a culturally informed intervention. *Journal of Consulting and Clinical Psychology*, 78(4), 449–58.

Katz, E. C., Brown, B. S., Schwartz, R. P., Weintraub, E., Barksdale, W., & Robinson, R. (2004). Role induction: A method for enhancing early retention in outpatient drug-free treatment. *Journal of Consulting and Clinical Psychology*, 72(2), 227–34

Klonoff, E. A., Landrine, H., & Ullman, J. B. (1996). Racial discrimination and psychiatric symptoms among blacks. *Cultural Diversity and Ethnic Minority Psychology*, 5(4), 329–39.

Koocher, G. P., & Keith-Spiegel, P. (2008). *Ethics in Psychology and the Mental Health Professions: Standards and Cases*. New York: Oxford University Press.

Korchin, S. J. (1980). Clinical psychology and minority problems. *American Psychologist*, 35(3), 262–69.

Kugelmass, H. (2016). "Sorry, I'm Not Accepting New Patients" An Audit Study of Access to Mental Health Care. *Journal of Health and Social Behavior*, 57(2), 168–83.

Liddle, H. A., Rowe, C. L., Dakof, G. A., Ungaro, R. A., & Henderson, C. E. (2004). Early intervention for adolescent substance abuse: Pretreatment to posttreatment outcomes of a randomized clinical trial comparing multidimensional family therapy and peer group treatment. *Journal of Psychoactive Drugs*, 36, 49–63.

Lowy, R. F. (1995). Eurocentrism, ethnic studies, and the new world order: Toward a critical paradigm. *Journal of Black Studies*, 25(6), 712–36.

Marterella, M. K., & Brock, L. J. (2008). Religion and spirituality as a resource in marital and family therapy. *Journal of Family Psychotherapy*, 19(4), 330–44.

May, C. L., & Wisco, B. E. (2016). Defining trauma: How level of exposure and proximity affect risk for posttraumatic stress disorder. *Psychological trauma: Theory, research, practice, and policy*, 8(2), 233–40.

McMiller, W. P., & Weisz, J. R. (1996). Help-seeking preceding mental health clinic intake among African-American, Latino, and Caucasian youths. *Journal of the American Academy of Child & Adolescent Psychiatry*, 35(8), 1086–94.

Morris, E. F. (2001). Clinical practices with African Americans: Juxtaposition of standard clinical practices and Africentricism. *Professional Psychology: Research and Practice*, 32(6), 563–72.

Nicolas, G., DaSilva, A., & Donnelly, S. (2011). *Social Networks and the Mental Health of Haitian Immigrants*. Coconut Cree, FL: Caribbean Studies Press.

Nicolas, G., Jean-Jacques, R., & Wheatley, A. (2012). Mental health counseling in Haiti: Historical overview, current status, and plans for the future. *Journal of Black Psychology*, 38(4), 509–19.

Obasi, E. M., & Leong, F. T. (2009). Psychological distress, acculturation, and mental health-seeking attitudes among people of African descent in the United States: A preliminary investigation. *Journal of Counseling Psychology*, 56(2), 227–38.

Obasi, E. M., & Leong, F. T. (2010). Construction and validation of the Measurement of Acculturation Strategies for People of African Descent (MASPAD). *Cultural Diversity and Ethnic Minority Psychology*, 16(4), 526–39.

Outlaw, F. H. (1993). Stress and Coping: The influence of racism the cognitive appraisal processing of African Americans. *Issues in Mental Health Nursing*, 14(4), 399–409.

Owen, J. J., Tao, K., Leach, M. M., & Rodolfa, E. (2011). Clients' perceptions of their psychotherapists' multicultural orientation. *Psychotherapy*, 48(3), 274–82.

Pieterse, A. L., Carter, R. T., & Ray, K. V. (2013). Racism-related stress, general life stress, and psychological functioning among Black American women. *Journal of Multicultural Counseling and Development*, 41(1), 36–46.

Pope, K. S., Tabachnick, B. G., & Keith-Spiegel, P. (1987). Ethics of practice: The beliefs and behaviors of psychologists as therapists. *American Psychologist*, 42(11), 993–1006.

Pope, K. S., & Vasquez, M. J. (2016). *Ethics in psychotherapy and counseling: A practical guide*. Hoboken, NJ: John Wiley & Sons.

Pope, K. S., & Vetter, V. A. (1992). Ethical dilemmas encountered by members of the American Psychological Association: A national survey. *American Psychologist*, *47*(3), 397–411.

Pope-Davis, D. B., Toporek, R. L., Ortega-Villalobos, L., Ligiéro, D. P., Brittan-Powell, C. S., Liu, W. M., Bashshur, M. R., Codrington, J. N., & Liang, C. T. (2002). Client perspectives of multicultural counseling competence: A qualitative examination. *The Counseling Psychologist*, *30*(3), 355–93.

Quintana, S. M. (2007). Racial and ethnic identity: Developmental perspectives and research. *Journal of Counseling Psychology*, *54*(3), 259–70.

Raja, A. (2016). Ethical considerations for therapists working with demographically similar clients. *Ethics & Behavior*, *26*(8), 678–87.

Randolph, S. M., & Banks, H. D. (1993). Making a way out of no way: The promise of Africentric approaches to HIV prevention. *Journal of Black Psychology*, *19*(2), 204–14.

Reverby, S. M. (2012). Ethical failures and history lessons: The U.S. Public Health Service research studies in Tuskegee and Guatemala. *Public Health Reviews*, *34*(1), 1–18.

Scurfield, R. M., & Mackey, D. W. (2001). Racism, trauma and positive aspects of exposure to race-related experiences: Assessment and treatment implications. *Journal of Ethnic and Cultural Diversity in Social Work*, *10*(1), 23–47.

Seaton, E. K., Caldwell, C. H., Sellers, R. M., & Jackson, J. S. (2008). The prevalence of perceived discrimination among African American and Caribbean Black youth. *Developmental Psychology*, *44*(5), 1288–97.

Sellers, R. M., & Shelton, J. N. (2003). The role of racial identity in perceived racial discrimination. *Journal of Personality and Social Psychology*, *84*(5), 1079–92.

Sinclair, C. (2017). Ethics in psychology: Recalling the past, acknowledging the present, and looking to the future. *Canadian Psychology*, *58*(1), 20–29.

Smith, T. B., & Trimble, J. E. (2016). *Foundations of Multicultural Psychology: Research to Inform Effective Practice*. Washington, DC: American Psychological Association.

Snowden, L. R. (2001). Barriers to effective mental health services for African Americans. *Mental Health Service Research*, *3*, 181–87.

Snowden, L. R., & Holschuh, J. (1992). Ethnic differences in emergency psychiatric care and hospitalization in a program for the severely mentally ill. *Community Mental Health Journal*, *28*(4), 281–91.

Snowden, L. R., Hu, T. W., & Jerrell, J. M. (1995). Emergency care avoidance: Ethnic matching and participation in minority-serving programs. *Community Mental Health Journal*, *31*(5), 463–73.

Substance Abuse and Mental Health Services Administration. (2015). *Racial/ Ethnic Differences in Mental Health Service Use among Adults*. HHS Publication No. SMA-15-4906. Rockville, MD: Author.

Sue, D. W., Arredondo, P., & McDavis, R. J. (1992). Multicultural counseling competencies and standards: A call to the profession. *Journal of Multicultural Counseling and Development*, *20*(2), 64–88.

Sue, D. W., Gallardo, M. E., & Neville, H. A. (2013). *Case Studies in Multicultural Counseling and Therapy*. New York: Wiley.

Sue, D. W., Nadal, K. L., Capodilupo, C. M., Lin, A. I., Torino, G. C., & Rivera, D. P. (2008). Racial microaggressions against Black Americans: Implications for counseling. *Journal of Counseling & Development*, *86*(3), 330–38.

Sue, S. (1998). In search of cultural competence in psychotherapy and counseling. *American Psychologist*, *53*(4), 440–48.

Sue, S. (2006). Cultural competency: From philosophy to research and practice. *Journal of Community Psychology*, *34*(2), 237–45.

Sue, S., Zane, N., Nagayama Hall, G. C., & Berger, L. K. (2009). The case for cultural competency in psychotherapeutic interventions. *Annual Review of Psychology*, *60*, 525–48.

Suite, D. H., La Bril, R., Primm, A., & Harrison-Ross, P. (2007). Beyond misdiagnosis, misunderstanding and mistrust: Relevance of the historical perspective in the medical and mental health treatment of people of color. *Journal of the National Medical Association*, 99(8), 879–85.

Tharinger, D., J., Finn, S. E., & Gentry, L. (2013). Therapeutic assessment with adolescents and their parents: A comprehensive model. In D. Saklofske, C. Reynolds, & V. Schwean (Eds.), *Oxford Handbook of Psychological Assessment of Children and Adolescents*. New York: Oxford University Press.

Tharinger, D. J., Finn, S. E., Gentry, L., Hamilton, A., Fowler, J., Matson, M., Krumholz, L., & Walkowiak, J. (2009). Therapeutic assessment with children: A pilot study of treatment acceptability and outcome. *Journal of Personality Assessment, 91*, 3, 238–44.

Tharinger, D. J., Finn, S. E., Wilkinson, A. D., & Schaber, P. M. (2007). Therapeutic assessment with a child as a family intervention: A clinical and research case study. *Psychology in the Schools, 44*(3), 293–309.

Thomas, S. B., & Quinn, S. C. (1991). The Tuskegee syphilis study, 1932–1972: Implications for HIV education and AIDS risk education programs in the Black community. *American Journal of Public Health, 81*(11), 1498–1505.

Thompson, C. E., & Jenal, S. T. (1994). Interracial and intraracial quasi-counseling interactions when counselors avoid discussing race. *Journal of Counseling Psychology, 41*(4), 484–91.

Thompson, V. L. S., & Alexander, H. (2006). Therapists' race and African American clients' reactions to therapy. *Psychotherapy: Theory, Research, Practice, Training, 43*(1), 99–110.

Thompson, R., Dancy, B. L., Wiley, T. R., Najdowski, C. J., Perry, S. P., Wallis, J., Mekawi, Y., & Knafl, K. A. (2013). African American families' expectations and intentions for mental health services. *Administration and Policy in Mental Health and Mental Health Services Research, 40*(5), 371–83.

Thompson, V. L. S. (1996). Perceived experiences of racism as stressful life events. *Community Mental Health Journal, 32*(3), 223–33.

Thompson, V. L. S., Bazile, A., & Akbar, M. (2004). African Americans' perceptions of psychotherapy and psychotherapists. *Professional Psychology: Research and Practice, 35*(1), 19–26.

Tiegreen, J. A., Braxton, L. E., Elbogen, E. B., & Bradford, D. (2012). Building a bridge of trust: Collaborative assessment with a person with serious mental illness. *Journal of Personality Assessment, 94*(5), 513–21.

Trimble, J. E., Scharrón-del Río, M., & Casillas, D. M. (2014). Ethical matters and contentions in the principled conduct of research with ethnocultural communities. In F. T. L. Leong (Ed.), *Handbook of Multicultural Psychology* (pp. 59–82). Washington, DC: American Psychological Association.

Turner, E. A. (2012). The parental attitudes toward psychological services inventory: Adaptation and development of an attitude scale. *Community Mental Health Journal, 48*(4), 436–49.

Turner, E. A., Cheng, H., Llamas, J., Tran, A. T., Hill, K., Fretts, J. M., & Mercado, A. (2016). Factors impacting the current trends in the use of outpatient psychiatric treatment among diverse ethnic groups. *Current Psychiatry Reviews, 12*(2), 199–220.

Turner, E. A., & Cherry, S. (2019, March). *Perceptions about accessing mental health services among African Americans and Latinos.* Poster presentation at the International Convention of Psychological Science. Paris, FR.

Turner, E. A., & Gamez, Y. (2018, April). *Racial differences in the role of religion and spirituality on decisions to use behavioral health treatment.* Poster presentation at the Society of Behavioral Medicine, New Orleans, LA.

Turner, E. A., & Liew, J. (2010). Children's adjustment and child mental health service use: The role of parents' attitudes and personal service use in an upper middle-class sample. *Community Mental Health Journal, 46*(3), 231–40.

Turner, E. A., Camarillo, J., Daniel, S., Otero, J., & Parker, A. (2017). Correlates of psychotherapy use among ethnically diverse college students. *Journal of College Student Development, 58*(2), 300–307.

Turner, E. A., Jensen-Doss, A., & Heffer, R. W. (2015). Ethnicity as a moderator of how parents' attitudes and perceived stigma influence intentions to seek child mental health services. *Cultural Diversity and Ethnic Minority Psychology*, 21(4), 613–18.

Turner, E. A., Malone, C., & Douglas, C. (2019). Barriers to mental health care for African Americans: Applying a model of treatment initiation to reduce disparities. In M. Williams, D. Rosen, & J. Kanter (Eds.), *Eliminating Race-Based Mental Health Disparities*. Oakland, CA: New Harbinger Press.

Turner, E. A., & Mills, C. (2016). Culturally relevant diagnosis and assessment of mental illness. In A., Breland-Noble, C., Al-Mateen, & N., Singh (Eds.), *Handbook of Mental Health in African American Youth* (pp. 21–35). New York: Springer International Publishing.

U.S. Department of Health and Human Services. (2001). Mental Health: Culture, Race, and Ethnicity—A Supplement to Mental Health: A Report of the Surgeon General. Rockville, MD: U.S. Department of Health and Human Services, Substance Abuse and Mental Health Services Administration, Center for Mental Health Services.

Utsey, S. O., & Payne, Y. (2000). Psychological impacts of racism in a clinical versus normal sample of African American men. *Journal of African American Men*, 5(3), 57–72.

Vasquez, M. J. (2012). Psychology and social justice: Why we do what we do. *American Psychologist*, 67(5), 337–46.

Wade, P., & Bernstein, B. L. (1991). Culture sensitivity training and counselor's race: Effects on Black female clients' perceptions and attrition. *Journal of Counseling Psychology*, 38(1), 9–15.

Webb, C. A., DeRubeis, R. J., & Barber, J. P. (2010). Therapist adherence/competence and treatment outcome: A meta-analytic review. *Journal of Consulting and Clinical Psychology*, 78(2), 200–11.

Webb, M. S. (2008). Does one size fit all African American smokers? The moderating role of acculturation in culturally specific interventions. *Psychology of Addictive Behaviors*, 22(4), 592–96.

Webb, M. S. (2009). Culturally specific interventions for African American smokers: An efficacy experiment. *Journal of the National Medical Association*, 101(9), 927–35.

Weinrach, S. G., & Thomas, K. R. (2004). The AMCD multicultural counseling competencies: A critically flawed initiative. *Journal of Mental Health Counseling*, 26(1), 81–93.

Weisz, J. R., & Weiss, B. (1991). Studying the "referability" of child clinical problems. *Journal of Consulting and Clinical Psychology*, 59(2), 266–73.

Whaley, A. L. (2001). Cultural Mistrust: An important psychological construct for diagnosis and treatment of African Americans. *Professional Psychology: Research and Practice*, 32(6), 555–62.

White, R. (2000). Unraveling the Tuskegee study of untreated syphilis. *Archives of Internal Medicine*, 160, 585–98.

Williams, M. T., Malcoun, E., Sawyer, B. A., Davis, D. M., Nouri, L. B., & Bruce, S. L. (2014). Cultural adaptations of prolonged exposure therapy for treatment and prevention of posttraumatic stress disorder in African Americans. *Behavioral Sciences*, 4(2), 102–24.

Williams, M. T., Metzger, I. W., Leins, C., & DeLapp, C. (2018). Assessing racial trauma within a DSM–5 framework: The UConn Racial/Ethnic Stress & Trauma Survey. *Practice Innovations*, 3(4), 242–60.

Williams, S. L. L. (2014). Mental health service use among African-American emerging adults, by provider type and recency of use. *Psychiatric Services*, 65(10), 1249–55.

Willis, M. G. (1989). Learning styles of African American children: A review of the literature and interventions. *Journal of Black Psychology*, 16(1), 47–65.

Worthington, R. L., Soth-McNett, A. M., & Moreno, M. V. (2007). Multicultural counseling competencies research: A 20-year content analysis. *Journal of Counseling Psychology*, 54(4), 351–61.

Yasui, M., Hipwell, A. E., Stepp, S. D., & Keenan, K. (2015). Psychocultural correlates of mental health service utilization among African American and European American girls. *Administration and Policy in Mental Health and Mental Health Services Research*, 42(6), 756–66.

Yorke, C. B., Voisin, D. R., & Baptiste, D. (2016). Factors related to help-seeking attitudes about professional mental health services among Jamaican immigrants. *International Social Work*, 59(2), 293–304.

INDEX

acculturation, 68
African American values, 60–65
African centered perspective. *See*
    Afrocentricism
Afrocentricism, 53, 58–60

barriers to treatment, 26–36
Black psychology, 35, 58–59, 64
Bryant-Davis, Thema, 12, 14, 15, 18

Caribbean psychology, 34, 50, 65–67. *See
    also* Jamaicans
Carter, Robert, 14–16, 22
client-therapist match, 31, 33, 50–51
clinical practice, 31, 39–54; treatment
    outcomes, 46–47. *See also* cultural
    competency
Cokley, Kevin, 14, 68
collaborative/therapeutic assessment, 73,
    74; conducting an assessment, 74, 75;
    research, 74–75
cultural competence, 21, 30, 39–46, 44,
    52–53
cultural competency. *See* multicultural
    competence
culturally adapted treatments, 49–50, 52,
    76, 78, 79; cultural adaptation models,
    77
culture, 31, 32, 36, 48

discrimination, 12, 28. *See also* racism

diversity in the profession, 32
Dudley-Grant, G. Rita, 59, 65

ethical principles, 7–8, 9
ethics, 2, 4; ethical violations, 34, 71;
    misconduct, 3; research, 4, 5
ethnic identity, 32, 59, 68

Ferguson shooting, 20

Goode-Cross, David, 72
Grills, Cheryl, 58
Guthrie, Robert, 1, 3

Helms, Janet, 15, 17

Jamaicans, 34, 35, 66–67

mental health: attitudes, 12; treatment
    seeking, 11
Model of Treatment Initiation, 25–26, 27,
    80
multicultural competence, 42, 43–46, 44,
    47
Myers, Linda James, 58

Nobles, Wade, 58
Nuremberg code, 4

Obasi, Ezemenari, 32, 68

police brutality, 13, 18–19, 20
post-traumatic stress disorder, 15, 20, 23

race-related stress, 14, 15, 17. *See also* racial trauma
racial socialization, 13, 23
racial trauma, 14, 16; assessment, 22; research, 14–21; treatment, 22–23
racism, 12; impacts on adults, 14; impacts on children and adolescents, 13, 18; types of racism, 12
religion, 36, 61
research, 3, 46–51; dismantling studies, 53; culturally adapted interventions, 77–80

Sellers, Robert, 18

Snowden, Lonnie, 26, 30
spirituality, 36, 61, 62–63
stigma, 35
Sue, Derald Wing, 39
Sue, Stanley, 39, 41, 51

Theory of Planned Behavior, 25–26
therapeutic alliance, 73–75
Turner, Erlanger, 25–26, 34, 35, 61, 72
Tuskegee study, 3, 34

Utsey, Shawn, 18

Vasquez, Melba, 4

Whaley, Arthur, 34
Williams, Monnica, 14–15, 22

ABOUT THE AUTHOR

Erlanger A. Turner, PhD, is a clinical psychologist and founder of Turner Psychological and Consulting Services, LLC. He has previously held faculty positions at Virginia Commonwealth University in the Department of Psychiatry and at the University of Houston-Downtown. His expertise includes behavioral parent training, cognitive-behavioral therapy, and psychological assessment. Dr. Turner has published research in peer-reviewed journals on behavioral health services, parental help-seeking behaviors, mental health among ethnic and racial groups, and psychometric evaluation of psychological measures. As a media psychologist, Dr. Turner has published a blog on *Psychology Today* called "The Race to Good Health" and contributed to a blog on the health section of *U.S. News & World Report*.

For over 10 years, Dr. Turner has served in numerous leadership roles within professional organizations. He has also served on the journal editorial board for *Practice Innovations*, *Psychological Services*, and *The Counseling Psychologist*. In 2014, he received the Judy E. Hall Early Career Psychologist Award by the National Register of Health Service Psychologists and served as the 2017 Chair of the American Psychological Association's Board for the Advancement of Psychology in the Public Interest. In 2016, he was appointed to the U.S. Department of Health and Human Services Behavioral Health Advisory committee to assist with the development and evaluation of an e-learning program for behavioral health providers (psychologists, social workers, and counselors) to improve providers' ability to work with individuals from diverse groups. Dr. Turner was also elected as the first African American male to serve as the president of the Society for Child and Family Policy and Practice in 2020 (Division 37 of the American Psychological Association).